Smart&Savvy

NEGOTIATION STRATEGIES IN ACADEMIA

Andrea Kupfer Schneider & David Kupfer

SmartSavvy**NEGOTIATION**.com

Smart & Savvy: Negotiation Strategies in Academia

Library of Congress Preassigned Control Number 2017913007

ISBN 9780999306109

Printed in the United States of America

Published by Meadows Communications LLC

Edited by Louisa Williams

Designed by Todd Germann

Table of Contents

Preface

This book is the product of a process of intergenerational learning and collaboration that started many years ago.

Here's how David Kupfer describes its origins:

The workings of the human mind—in particular, how and why people think and behave in particular ways—caught my interest early on, dating back to when I was a high school student growing up on Long Island, but I never considered that interest could be the basis of a career. Like many young men of my generation, I had my heart set on becoming a physician, and all my energies were focused in that direction. It wasn't until my second year of medical school, when I encountered a charismatic psychiatrist who was arguing that the brain could be studied like any other organ of the body, that I actually considered a career in psychiatry. After studying and teaching at Yale University and the National Institute of Mental Health, focusing on understanding, diagnosing, and treating mood disorders, I moved to Pittsburgh to become Director of Research under the chairmanship of that same charismatic teacher who had first sparked my interest in psychiatry as a science. Eventually, I became chair of that department and saw it become the national leader in research funding and home to more than 200 highly successful faculty members.

As the years passed, and as we recruited more young people to join the department at Pitt, I found myself increasingly serving as a mentor, helping others navigate the path to success in academic medicine. Trainees and young faculty members sought me out, asking for various kinds of help. The questions were often about their scientific hypotheses, how best to frame their research questions, how to understand the outcomes of their studies, and how best to present those outcomes, both in person and in writing, but just as often their questions involved career concerns. What should a young female resident do about timing her next pregnancy when she feels the biological clock ticking but wants to take on a particularly demanding set of rotations because they seem essential to her career goals? How should a young faculty member who has just received his first research grant begin to gracefully establish his independence from the chief of his laboratory, who still sees him as someone to boss around?

As these conversations continued, I started to turn my attention to career development, which led to the articulation of a pathway of steps along the road to academic success and then to the creation of formal courses in career development, an interest that has now captured my imagination for more than 30 years. Working on these career development programs, I noticed a startling gap: unlike their business and law school peers, academics generally receive no training in negotiation skills. This made no sense to me: studies show that young scientists often fall off their career paths because they weren't satisfied— but that the lack of satisfaction generally is less about science than it is about interpersonal challenges and workplace communication.

At about this time, my oldest daughter, Andrea, and her professional work as a law professor engaged in the teaching of negotiation provided a chance to collaborate on a solution.

Andrea Kupfer Schneider picks up the story.

Growing up as the oldest of four, I feel as if I negotiated a lot. Sometimes it was to get what I wanted; other times, on behalf of my younger siblings. I did not originally think about law as a career, but a summer in college, working for my beloved grandfather, who in his law career seemed to have figured out a terrific balance between work and family and community, intrigued me. I went off to law school expecting to focus on international transactions or international diplomacy.

Then in my first year, I took a negotiation class that opened my eyes to the theory behind skillful communication and challenged me to address my own weaknesses (or at least become aware of them). I was smitten: negotiation and dispute resolution quickly became the central focus of my law school studies, with more classes, internships, and articles. I was a research and teaching assistant during law school at Harvard and worked with Roger Fisher, one of the founders of the field. Right after graduation, I was then able to teach at Stanford Law School with another giant in the field, Robert Mnookin.

Although I returned to the East and practiced law for two years, more than 20 years ago I was delighted to get back to teaching full time and then to move to Marquette University Law School, where I teach alternative dispute resolution, negotiation, ethics, and international conflict resolution. I also have continually trained people on negotiation skills in businesses, law firms, nonprofits, and other entities. As I have made my way through the academic maze to getting tenure and directing the dispute resolution program, I often turned to friends, family, and mentors, including my father, for advice. His guidance, I found, was useful across disciplines and departments.

Over the years, as my father and I discussed both what I was teaching and what he was working on, we agreed that I would do some training for his career development program. The response to that two-hour training almost a decade ago was extremely positive, and it has kept us working together ever since.

As we began to lead career development programs for young people pursuing academic research careers, we quickly realized how central negotiation skills are to academic success, a recognition that is embodied in the recent grant renewal for the joint career development training program in psychiatry and neuroscience at the University of Pittsburgh and Stanford University that we run. The demand for negotiation training continues to grow; today, for students enrolled in the program, we offer six hours of classroom activity, a webinar, and in-person meetings over the course of the year.

To our great pleasure, the reviews have been glowing. The negotiation training really worked, participants tell us, and because of what they learned they feel more confident asking for what they need to be successful. Even when they don't get what they need, they say, now they can step back, analyze what happened, diagnose the situation, and strategize about how to improve for the next negotiation. In short, knowing more about negotiation has given them confidence that their skills can improve over time. As they left school and negotiated in their workplaces, graduates of the career development program asked us for more advanced training, and my father and I have been busy with tutorials, trainings, and lectures in medical schools and many other university venues.

In more than 10 years of helping academics and scientists learn about negotiation, many of our participants have urged us to write a book that presents a framework for mastering negotiation skills and provides a pathway to improving such skills over time through practice and experience. We initially thought of writing a book for early career academics in medicine, but after much discussion—between us, with our colleagues, with former students, and others—we shifted to creating something more broadly applicable to different contexts and different life stages. We understand that no one book can be all things to all people, but we aim to address a wide audience of professionals at varying stages in their careers.

How did my father and I negotiate the writing of this book? The process has been shockingly smooth, with only a few disagreements and many (mostly expected) challenges created by the obligations of two adults who are busy with work, partners, children, grandchildren, friends, and fun (which includes travel and downhill skiing). Our negotiation styles? Maybe some fathers and daughters compete or accommodate, but the best description of our style is collaborative; one of us creates a chapter or has an idea, sends it to the other, he or she responds with suggestions, and we talk. This book, as we said at the start, is the product of two people who share many common interests—and also much mutual respect for each of our areas of expertise.

We hope that in reading this book you will learn about negotiation styles and effectiveness, increase your self-understanding through the assessment tools in the appendices, think about how you would handle the challenges posed in the scenarios, and, most important, start to practice your negotiation skills. Becoming an effective negotiator is a journey, and we look forward to hearing about yours.

— Andrea Kupfer Schneider and David Kupfer
July, 2017

CHAPTER 1
Where You Start

Introduction

Negotiating your way through academia effectively and smoothly, like any skill, requires both knowledge and practice. And just like any other skill, negotiating is something you will develop in your own way, adding onto your existing tendencies, talents, and strengths. With this in mind, before you start thinking about negotiation skills, take a look at your own baseline skills and preferred styles. What are your strengths? Are you an attentive listener, for instance? Can you think quickly on your feet? Are you an especially careful researcher? What about your comfort zone? Are you happiest in a small office, with no disturbances, or do you shine bright at big parties? What interactions that might throw other people are relatively easy for you?

Like all of us, by the time you started your career you had developed certain habits of communication. You now have ways of expressing yourself that you accumulated over many years, long enough that many of the habits became ingrained. Some might come from your original family—large or small, loud or quiet, a group in which conflicts were discussed openly, smoothed over, or ignored. Some might come from activities you chose—team or individual sports, strategy games, or debate. Some probably come from your professional choices; if your academic experience has been a typical social or hard-science one, advocacy for yourself was not a major part of your professional or formal curriculum, as it would have been in law school or business school.

Of course, many of your communication habits simply come from your personality and temperament. If you are outgoing, making a point on your behalf in a conversation probably comes easily. If you tend to stay back and listen, you are probably good at reading other people's signals and understanding what motivates them.

Other skills have developed in response to what has worked for you in the past. All of us know people who seem not to have progressed much past their toddler personality, at least in terms of negotiation, those who assume that if they throw a hissy fit, they will get their way. As we hope you will discover through this book, in the adult world, most of the time other behaviors will be more effective for getting what you want.

Take a moment now and reflect on how you communicate to get what you want. Your style probably changes based on the context of the negotiation and with whom you are negotiating. Different situations call for different styles, and your style can—and may need to—change to during the course of a single negotiation, from when conflict first arises to when it intensifies. You are negotiating every time you are trying to change someone's mind or get someone to do something differently. So you probably have developed a set of habits over time that may—or may not—work effectively in various contexts. But understanding negotiation and developing your own negotiation skills will enable you to navigate difficult interpersonal situations to move your career forward. When competing for jobs, for resources, and for salaries, professionals who are effective negotiators have a huge advantage.[1]

Although people often criticize someone's style (as pushy or passive aggressive or even obnoxious, say) there is no "right" or "wrong" style; there's only the most effective style for the particular situation. Compromising, for example, isn't always wise, and avoiding isn't always cowardly. Instead, think of different styles as different strategies you can use as needed. How do you deal with your siblings or parents when planning holiday celebrations or vacation together? How do you and your friends decide what movie to see or where to go to dinner? How do you handle asking your roommate for rent payments or to do a better job cleaning up? What about when you and your romantic partner disagree? And how do you negotiate at work? Does your approach vary depending on whether you're talking to a colleague, a boss, or a research assistant? Certainly it does—and that's a good thing.

Step one in this book will be to raise your awareness about different approaches to negotiation that are available to you—and point out that you probably already use several of them.

Step two will be to highlight the skills necessary to execute each approach. You probably choose how to negotiate based on your already-existing skill set. In other words, if you are good at listening, you will be good at finding out what other people want and at making them happy. If you are not comfortable advocating for yourself, on the other hand, you probably will not choose to negotiate in a more competitive way. To be able to choose from a larger range of styles in any one situation, you will need to build specific skills.

After outlining styles and skills, this book offers scenarios you can use to practice, to try out your responses. The point of the book, after all, is to help you negotiate in the academic world—not to explain all the nuances of negotiation theory. Later chapters cover the following academic challenges and milestones:

- Mentorship: Choosing a mentor and mentoring over the "career cycle"
- PhD Thesis (or the equivalent advanced degree)
- Fellowship/Post-Doctoral Training
- Authorship
- Separation: Getting a Divorce from Your Mentor—and Surviving
- First Faculty Appointment
- First Grant Award
- Promotion and Advancement
- Tenure
- Retirement

You will find several exercises and questionnaires in the appendix that social scientists have developed over decades and we have adapted for use in this book. Each should be useful in helping you learn initially about your default approach to conflict and then focusing on each of the skills that we will examine in more detail in the first few chapters of the book. These are designed so that you can fill out each exercise as you go through the book to give you more specific information about yourself and your skills.

So let's get started. Complete the DYNAD exercise, a tool Andrea developed to measure responses to conflict.[2] The Dynamic Negotiating Approach Diagnostic asks you to assess yourself at the start of a conflict and then again after the conflict becomes more difficult. Once you have scored your results, turn to Chapter Two for discussion of the advantages and disadvantages of each style.

DYNAMIC NEGOTIATING APPROACH DIAGNOSTIC (DYNAD)

INSTRUCTIONS: Consider your response in situations where your wishes differ from those of another person. Note that statements A-J deal with your _initial_ response to disagreement; statements K-T deal with your response _after the disagreement has gotten stronger_. For consistency, choose one particular conflict setting and use it as background for all the questions. Note that there are no "right" or "wrong" answers; your first impression is usually best. _What the Test Means & How to Score It: page 160_

Circle one number on the line below each statement for questions A through T.

<- Not at all Characteristic   Very Characteristic ->

A. WHEN I FIRST DISCOVER THAT DIFFERENCES EXIST,
I make sure that all views are out in the open and treated with equal consideration, even if there seems to be substantial disagreement.

1	2	3	4	5	6

B. WHEN I FIRST DISCOVER THAT DIFFERENCES EXIST,
I devote more attention to making sure others understand the logic and benefits of my position than I do to pleasing them.

1	2	3	4	5	6

C. WHEN I FIRST DISCOVER THAT DIFFERENCES EXIST,
I make my needs known, but I tone them down a bit and look for solutions somewhere in the middle.

1	2	3	4	5	6

D. WHEN I FIRST DISCOVER THAT DIFFERENCES EXIST,
I delay talking about the issue until I have had time to think it over.

1	2	3	4	5	6

E. WHEN I FIRST DISCOVER THAT DIFFERENCES EXIST,
I devote more attention to the feelings of others than to expressing my personal concerns.

1	2	3	4	5	6

F. WHEN I FIRST DISCOVER THAT DIFFERENCES EXIST,
I am more concerned with goals I believe to be important than with how others feel about the issue.

1	2	3	4	5	6

G. WHEN I FIRST DISCOVER THAT DIFFERENCES EXIST,
I often realize that trying to resolve the differences are not worth my effort.

1	2	3	4	5	6

H. WHEN I FIRST DISCOVER THAT DIFFERENCES EXIST,
I make sure my goals do not get in the way of our relationship.

1	2	3	4	5	6

I. WHEN I FIRST DISCOVER THAT DIFFERENCES EXIST,
I actively explain my ideas and just as actively take steps to understand others' ideas.

1	2	3	4	5	6

J. WHEN I FIRST DISCOVER THAT DIFFERENCES EXIST,
I give up some points in exchange for others.

1	2	3	4	5	6

K. IF DIFFERENCES PERSIST AND FEELINGS OF CONFLICT ESCALATE,
I set aside my own preferences and become more concerned with keeping the relationship comfortable.

1	2	3	4	5	6

L. IF DIFFERENCES PERSIST AND FEELINGS OF CONFLICT ESCALATE,
I refocus discussions and hold out for ways to meet the needs of others as well as my own.

1	2	3	4	5	6

M. IF DIFFERENCES PERSIST AND FEELINGS OF CONFLICT ESCALATE,
I let others handle the problem.

1	2	3	4	5	6

N. IF DIFFERENCES PERSIST AND FEELINGS OF CONFLICT ESCALATE,
I try to be reasonable by not asking for my full preferences and I make sure I get some of what I want.

1	2	3	4	5	6

O. IF DIFFERENCES PERSIST AND FEELINGS OF CONFLICT ESCALATE,
I put forth greater effort to make sure that the truth as I see it is recognized and less on pleasing others.

1	2	3	4	5	6

P. IF DIFFERENCES PERSIST AND FEELINGS OF CONFLICT ESCALATE,
I interact less with others and look for ways to find a safe distance.

1	2	3	4	5	6

Q. IF DIFFERENCES PERSIST AND FEELINGS OF CONFLICT ESCALATE,
I press for moderation and compromise so we can make a decision and move on.

1	2	3	4	5	6

R. IF DIFFERENCES PERSIST AND FEELINGS OF CONFLICT ESCALATE,
I do what needs to be done to resolve the conflict in my favor and hope we can mend feelings later.

1	2	3	4	5	6

S. IF DIFFERENCES PERSIST AND FEELINGS OF CONFLICT ESCALATE,
I do what is necessary to soothe the other's feelings.

1	2	3	4	5	6

T. IF DIFFERENCES PERSIST AND FEELINGS OF CONFLICT ESCALATE,
I pay close attention to the wishes of others but remain firm that they need to pay equal attention to my wishes.

1	2	3	4	5	6

FLEXIBLITY
EMPATHY
assertiveness

CHAPTER 2
Styles of Negotiation

Negotiation theorists have identified at least five key styles people use in a conflict or negotiation.[3] For the purposes of this book, we first describe each style, its advantages, and its disadvantages, and then discuss what skills you need to implement each one. We also look at the role of goals—what you want to accomplish in the negotiation—and how that determines which style you select.

The following chart, developed by Andrea based on the original Thomas-Kilmann Conflict Mode Instrument,[4] details each style along three axes—level of assertiveness, level of empathy, and level of flexibility (or effort and creativity) needed to implement the style. In Chapter 3, we will come back to these axes to discuss the skills needed to move up and down each one.

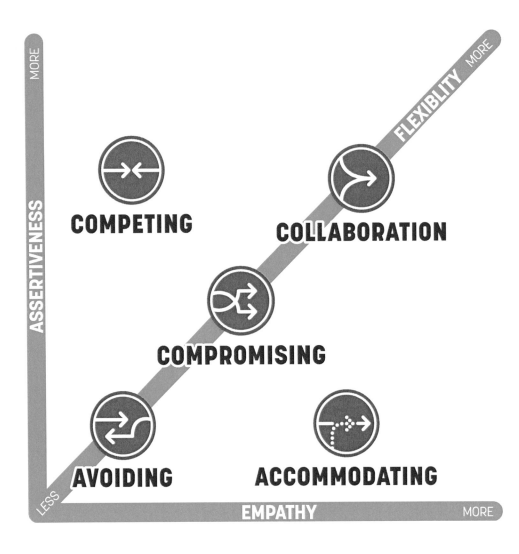

COMPETING

Competing is probably the most commonly understood style of negotiation because it is the one most of us mastered at age 2 (and some of us never moved past). Because competing tends to be dramatic, it makes good theater and good stories. Because we so often see people competing—on the playing field, on the movie screen, and in the political arena, you might think, mistakenly, that this is how most conflicts are resolved. It's not. In real life, most disagreements are resolved through communication and problem-solving.[5] But before celebrating or condemning competing, let's understand a little more about what it comprises.

A competing strategy is high in assertiveness and low in empathy, probably also low on flexibility. To compete effectively, you must make a strong case for yourself, you must be persuasive and firm, and you must often appear to be taking charge or controlling the conversation. The power of this style is the clarity of your position, and often the persuasiveness and the knowledge that goes along with being convinced that you are correct.

The advantages of competing are clear: if you come on strong, the other side might agree with you right off the bat and you might get your way with relatively little effort. Competing can be efficient: if you get your way within minutes, you don't waste much time. And in many cases, after a successful resolution, everyone understands who won and what was decided.

Of course, we all know the downsides of too much competing. If you approach a battle looking for a fight and convinced that you will win, the other side might not agree and might fight back even harder than he or she would if you took a softer approach, which can damage your relationship or lead to stalemate—or both. Some people might refuse to work with colleagues who are unceasingly competitive. And, less obvious but just as important, someone in power who is overly competitive, perhaps a team leader, could lose the valuable input of team members who tire of the "my-way-or-the-highway" style of decision-making.

Under what circumstances is competing a great choice? It's effective when important values (such as safety or reputation) are at stake, when a quick decision is needed (for example, when a deadline is approaching or a decision is urgent), or when you know the other side is likely to give up easily.

ACCOMMODATING

At the opposite spectrum of behavior is the accommodating style of negotiation. This is low assertiveness and high empathy usually characterized by quickly agreeing to what the other side wants. This results in "giving in," agreeing and supporting the other side. The power behind this style is that if your greatest concern is making the other side happy, accommodating accomplishes that quickly and completely—as long as the other side approves.

Accommodating offers distinct advantages: If you give in, the other side will probably appreciate your bowing to his or her wishes, and that could improve your relationship. It also eliminates the conflict (at least in the short term) and can be efficient and easy to implement. You just say yes.

The big disadvantage to an accommodating style is that you don't get what you want. There are other drawbacks: other people might be frustrated by your lack of input, especially when they do want to work with you, or might lose respect for you and your interests. If you accommodate everyone all the time, a reputation of always giving in can damage your relationships and can make it increasingly difficult for you to stand up for yourself. It also denies you and your counterpart the opportunity to work through conflict in a productive manner.

An accommodating style is a good choice in several situations. If you really don't care about something (what movie to see, say, or where to go for dinner), giving in is simple. It works well when you care more about the relationship than the topic under discussion ("I have no interest in going to the opera, but if you want to go, I'll go with you.") Accommodating can also be used as part of a package of trade-offs. ("You decide this time. Next time, the choice is mine.") The catch in using accommodating as a relationship builder or as a trade-off is to be sure to communicate that accommodating *now* is connected to the *future*; if you fail to do that, the other person might not understand that sometime down the road, he or she must accommodate you.

AVOIDING Moving to another corner, avoiding is low assertiveness and low empathy as well as low creativity and flexibility. It also has the lowest level of energy devoted to dealing with the conflict. Think of avoiding as both a long-term (stick your head in the sand) and short-term (don't answer the email until later) type of strategy. You are delaying or avoiding a response to a conflict, trying to divert attention, not signaling how you really feel about a particular situation, and suppressing your personal emotion and position about this conflict.

The key advantage to avoiding is the lack of entanglement in issues that are trivial to you or relationships that are not sufficiently significant. Avoiding can freeze the status quo. And the conflict might be solved without your input. Most crucially, avoiding is a necessary component of time management and sanity maintenance (such as not answering your phone when caller ID shows it's from a marketing firm or long-winded friend). Not every problem needs you to solve it, and not every conflict is worthy of your energy. You might be wise, for example, to discuss with your department chair only the issues that are really hindering your research. Ignoring or avoiding other concerns allows both you and your negotiation partner to distinguish between the annoying and the important.

On the other hand, if you use this strategy too often or for too long, the disadvantages can be notable. People—you as well as others—might periodically explode from frustration. You could be frozen out from discussions on some matters, and others could feel negatively about your avoidance. If the problem gets solved without your input—and perhaps it will not be—you will not be participating in the solution that gets implemented.

So do think about when to avoid. For issues that you consider trivial or in situations where you know that others will take the lead and you will not mind, avoidance makes sense. Avoiding also is useful when you are not yet ready to negotiate. Perhaps you need more time to research the situation and figure out how to approach it. Perhaps you are too busy to really focus on the conflict. Perhaps you need to schedule the conversation for a time when you can be emotionally prepared. All of these are smart reasons for delaying your own engagement until you can be most effective.

COLLABORATION

At the last corner of the grid is collaborating, a strategy that engages the most energy by requiring assertiveness, empathy, and creativity for resolving the situation. If accommodating means "yes—we'll do it your way," collaborating is characterized by a "yes and …" style, one in which you clearly state your preference while also inquiring about the preference of the other side. The strategy is problem-focused, and multiple points of view are welcome in thinking about how to solve the dispute. The power of this style is in the complete involvement of everyone present—the ownership of the group—and potentially integrative, imaginative solutions.

The advantages to collaborating are primarily located in your relationship with the other party and in the substance of the solution. First, because the parties work together in creating the solution, they build trust between them. Because the dynamic of working together is often energetic and cooperative, collaborating increases the chances that the relationship will be improved and that the solution will be carried out. Second, because people's perspectives have been merged and they have probably shared more ideas in the collaborative process, any solution they devise is likely to be based on sound, relevant information and to be more durable than one that was decided unilaterally.

On the other hand, collaborating can be exhausting. Working with others takes time and motivation, can distract those involved from other pressing problems, and can bring on "analysis paralysis," a state in which too many people spend too much time analyzing and not enough time deciding. Especially when several parties are involved, just trying to enlist everyone in a collaborative process can take longer than the issue is worth.

In deciding when to collaborate, a negotiator needs to think about how important the issue is, how helpful information from the other side might be in figuring out a good solution, and how valuable the relationship with the other party or parties is. When done effectively, collaborating can merge the best of all possible worlds and is often the gold standard of how research and clinical work is done. At the same time, not every dispute is worth this level of attention.

COMPROMISING

Finally, in the middle of all of these styles is compromising, a strategy characterized by finding middle ground and using some empathy and creativity. A compromising style will urge moderation; use techniques like split-the-difference or trade-off, and move the parties toward finding a solution that offers something for everyone.

The advantages to compromising are numerous—it can be relatively fast, it can move things forward and give parties a way out of a stalemate, it is easy to understand and implement, and it appears reasonable. It is also familiar, because ever since childhood, when we had to take turns and share toys, most of us have long understood compromise as structurally fair.

On the other hand, when it is not moored to standards, compromising can feel like horse-trading. If we move to agreement and to creating a solution too quickly, it can be at the expense of better and more well thought-out answers, and we may miss a chance to hear everyone's point of view. Compromising can also lead to patching up the symptoms of conflict without dealing with the causes, which can mean that the conflict will flare again.

Compromise is best used in two instances—when the issues are relatively unimportant to all concerned and an easy, efficient trade-off ("You pick the restaurant; I'll pick the movie") makes sense. Compromising is also an excellent "second-choice" style to conflict. At the end of a collaborating style, when few issues remain, compromising can get the deal done. And if competing is leading to what could be a stalemate, compromising can move the agenda forward.

* * *

Like a barometer, successful negotiators tend to shift from one style to another as new information is presented. In self-assessing yourself, however, be aware of how you tend to approach negotiation before conflict arises—your preferred "calm" style—and how you tend to respond if conflict intensifies—your preferred "storm" style. As the DYNAD exercise shows, these results may vary with the conflict situation you have in mind. (In fact, you can take the DYNAD again, thinking of a different context than the one you used initially to see if this may be true for you.) Understanding your calm and storm style can help you better understand your natural tendencies when negotiating and which styles you're most inclined to use. (If you took the DYNAD, you will see that you might shift as the conflict heats up.)

You will note that each of the styles requires you to have some level of skill to execute it satisfactorily. As we indicated earlier, the key to successful negotiation includes understanding your preferred styles as well as being able to shift styles strategically based on your accurate interpretation of the negotiation context and climate. Negotiation styles are never static; they often change over time and as conditions and information develop. After we discuss preparation in Chapter 3, in Chapters 4 through 7, we will discuss the skills of assertiveness, empathy, and flexibility, look at how you can build your skill repertoire, and examine that priceless instinct called social intuition, which will help you determine which style to use in any situation. Then in the next three Chapters, 8 through 10, we will show how these skills are implemented. Chapter 8 will discuss the issues of trust and reputation in negotiation; Chapter 9 turns to the question of how we should be communicating given all of the current choices technology provides; and then Chapter 10 places all of this in a multi-party context, to understand how these negotiations—among lab partners or multiple coauthors or at a faculty meeting—also benefit from careful and strategic thinking.

INTERESTS

goals priorities

context

CHAPTER 3

Preparation

President Abraham Lincoln once said, "I will prepare and some day my chance will come."[6] And, more recently, basketball coach John Wooden noted, "Failing to prepare is preparing to fail."[7] How can you prepare for a negotiation? And, even when you understand the various styles of negotiating—and which ones you favor—how do you decide when to use which one?

Here's where your research skills will come in handy. Just like crafting an effective experimental design, putting together a cohesive narrative for a manuscript, or writing a grant application, getting what you want through negotiation requires preparation. As you prepare, three questions will help you choose and shape your strategy:

- What do you want?
- What do you think the other party wants?
- What are the circumstances or context surrounding the negotiation?

At this stage, it's helpful to think about the difference between "positions" and "interests,"[8] a distinction that isn't always obvious to everyone in a negotiation. In a conversation with your boss or chair, for instance, your stated position might be that you want a raise. You want more money, and you want it immediately. (In negotiations, especially contentious ones, people often start off by emphatically stating their positions, which then leads the other party to state his or her opposing position with equal vehemence.) And remember, positions can be tactical moves that are used to disguise or underemphasize the longer-term goals or major interests for the outcome. Interests, however, are what you need or most want out of the negotiation. Your interests behind your position, that you want a raise, are more nuanced—perhaps you are looking for financial security, fairness (you want to be paid what you know is the market rate), respect from the chair, or recognition for a successful year. Maybe your interests are a blend of all those. Note that interests can be tangible, like money or a more comfortable workspace, or intangible, like respect or parity. Once you have identified your interests, you should figure out your priorities, ranking your interest by what's most important to you. At the same time, you should try to guess what might be important to the other person or people you will be negotiating with.

Knowing what you want—and why—is critical, but this knowledge alone isn't enough. Next comes the challenge of setting goals and attaching specific ideas to your interests, which is a crucial step for getting what you want. Having specific goals, as opposed to vague ones, can help you focus and stay patient in the negotiation toward achieving your interests.[9] Making your goals ambitious or aspirational is also important: If you ask for something you know the other person will give, your success rate will be high. But if you really want to accomplish more—to get more resources to meet your needs or achieve your professional goals, for example—you need to aim high.[10]

Your goals need another attribute: reasonableness. If you want to succeed in negotiation, your goals should be justifiable to yourself and to the person (or people) across the table. This has double advantages: if you consider your own goals fair, based on reasonable criteria, you will be more likely to feel good about asking them, and if the person across the table understands the reasoning behind what you are asking for, he or she will be more likely to give you what you want.[11]

Returning to that negotiation with your boss or chair for a raise, here's how you might organize and break down your preparation well in advance of any actual conversation:

Be Specific

1   Define your goal. State who (or what institution) is involved, what you want to accomplish, why it's important to you, and how you're going to make it happen. For example, "I want a salary of $110,000 for a junior faculty position at the research university that has extended me a job offer. This is an increase of $10,000 from the starting offer."

2   Make sure you can measure progress toward your goal. Break up your action plan into steps.[12] For example, "I will make a list of my supporting arguments as well as the potential counterarguments and then practice discussing them to prepare for negotiating in person or over the phone." (How to make these arguments will be covered in the next chapter.)

3   Set a deadline for yourself. Having a time frame will help motivate you to take action. For example, "I have two weeks to respond to their offer, so I will schedule this conversation with my chair for next week."

Be Reasonable

Be sure to pursue goals that are well founded in standards and practices. When your goals are based on objective criteria and your arguments are fair and justified, your arguments will be more persuasive—to you as well as the other person. For example, "Junior faculty with a comparable amount of research experience average $110,000 in salary at this university and similar institutions."

Be Aspirational and Optimistic

Pick a goal that's at the high end of what is justifiable and fair. Negotiators who set optimistic goals achieve better results for two reasons: They are more patient, more willing to go back and forth, while pursuing their goals. They also "anchor," or provide a firm foundation, for the discussion at a high point, perhaps a point that is higher than the other party might have considered. For example, "I will start by asking for a salary of $125,000, which is at the high end of the university's salary range for junior faculty, and negotiate from there."

***

After you've created your specific, reasonable, and aspirational goals, you'll need to gather the information you need to develop support for your position. For example, if you're negotiating the terms of your first job offer, you'll want to know the standard salary, benefits, and workload for the position. Doing your research will prepare you to justify your interests clearly and persuasively.

To be clear, this is both the easiest and perhaps the most time-consuming part of negotiation. It is the easiest because you alone control the amount of time and energy that you put into preparation. Unlike every other step in negotiation, when you will have to rely on the other person or other people to meet your goals, at this stage you're the only player. The more you know and prepare, the more confident and the more creative you can be. This also means that your chances of figuring out the next step of how to meet the interests of the person or people you will be negotiating with are also improved. Because doing this well requires considerable time and effort, effective negotiators always factor in preparation time when they schedule the actual negotiation session.

Next you'll need to look at the other side's perspective. What are his, her, or their goals? Try to find out in advance what they might want, and think about how you can use your talents and contributions as leverage or to make trade-offs with their interests. You may have more bargaining chips than you realize. If possible, try to verify any assumptions you may have about their position with other people. Researching the other side will help you accurately anticipate their arguments and their responses to yours. (You'll learn more about how to understand the other side in the chapter on empathy.)

Look for places where your interests overlap—the best solutions are often the ones that come closest to meeting everyone's needs. You'll also need to consider what each party's alternatives might be if the negotiation isn't successful.[13] If, for example, your chair has several other junior faculty to hire, will that mean less budgeted money available to you? Or might the chair worry about limited lab space? (You'll learn more about creating options in the chapter on flexibility and about how to determine your best alternative, or bottom line, in the chapter on assertiveness.)

You'll also need to assess the context surrounding the negotiation. Will you be under time pressure to accept any offer? Might the other side be under pressure to hire quickly as well? Which negotiation styles and skills you decide to use will depend on the personalities and relationships involved as well as the setting and the typical ways that negotiations are conducted.

All this advance thinking and research may seem like a lot of work, but it will be worth the effort. Preparing your negotiation strategy will help clarify your own position, give you a better understanding of the other side, and increase your awareness of additional factors that could influence the negotiation. (For each of the scenarios in later chapters, you'll find lists of possible goals, intended to help you see how this works in practice.)

What follows is a table to help you prepare for any negotiation. You may not be able to answer every question fully, and that is okay. Just trying to address these as much you can will help you be more confident, more prepared and more effective.

The Situation

What are you negotiating for and with whom?

	YOU	THEM	IN CONTEXT
Interests	What do you want?	What do they want?	What are your common interests?
Persuasion & Criteria	What are your arguments?	What are their arguments?	What are the counter-arguments?
Trade-offs	What do you have that they need?	What do they have that you need?	What are you willing and able to give them? What options can you propose?
Alternatives	What are your other alternatives?	What are their other alternatives?	What will you do if the negotiation doesn't go well?
Relationship	What is your relationship to them?	What is their relationship to you?	How might this negotiation help or harm the relationship?
Style	Which style do you prefer?	Which style are they most likely to use?	Which style would serve you best?

Rating Your Trails

EASIEST   INTERMEDIATE   EXPERT

Your level of needed skills will depend on both the context and your counterpart. To help think through this, consider skiing as an analog. As you probably know, ski trails are rated according to difficulty. In fact, Disney created a standardized system in the 1960s (when it was contemplating building a ski resort) and wanted clear and standard signage for its patrons. Before that time, each resort used its own set of signage. Under our now-standard US signage, green circles generally designate easy ski routes that have a slope under 25 degrees, offer a wide path for turns, and are well groomed. Blue squares are intermediate routes—a steeper slope, perhaps less room to maneuver, and some bumps or moguls along the way. Black diamonds designate yet more challenging routes down the mountain, very steep trails with a pitch greater than 45 degrees. They might not be groomed, will probably have moguls, and can have other hazards such as drop-offs or trees. Double black diamond trails are the most challenging trails on the mountain, with all of the above—they are full of moguls, often narrow, very steep, and have dangerous hazards.

This analogy works well for a number of reasons. First, all slopes will get you to the bottom of the mountain, one way or another. You may be able to point your skis straight down and go full speed ahead, or you might—at the other extreme—take off your skis and walk down at the trail's edge. Whichever route or mode of moving you choose, at the end of the day, you will get to the bottom of the mountain. Which leads to the next similarity between skiing and negotiating (and with what you have to do in your work and in your life): you will probably take the lift up the mountain and ski down again. The next interaction may be on a trail that is more difficult or easier than the one you just took—or you might want to take the same trail again, now that you are familiar with it, and continue to improve your skills.

Ski trail ratings and negotiation types share another attribute: Although different ski resorts in the United States all use this rating system (in Europe and Japan, some resorts add another gradation and some use red for intermediate slopes) and all resorts rate their own trails consistently, not all resorts rate the slopes the same. In other words, one resort in Vermont will mark all its most difficult trails with a black diamond or two, but a trail that rates a black diamond in Vermont may be a blue square in Colorado. Or a green circle in Utah might be rated as a blue square in Wisconsin. So although you will find consistent signs at any one resort, those systems aren't always transferrable to other areas. In short, local cultures and local attitudes matter, which is why you will want to be aware of context in each of your negotiations.

Also, each of us has our own degree of skill and our own perception of difficult, our own definitions of black diamonds and green circles. What is easy for you to ask for might make your colleague (or your chair or your next-door neighbor) break out in a cold sweat (and vice versa). Depending on the context and the counterpart, every negotiation interaction will have a different degree of difficulty, different bumps and moguls, and different hazards. Success in navigating your way down the mountain comes from knowing your own skills and hopes, being keenly aware of current conditions, and understanding your counterpart's needs and abilities.

CHAPTER 4
Assertiveness

Why is assertiveness so important to negotiation? Effective negotiators know how to ask for what they want. They know how to frame their arguments in a way that will be persuasive, they know how to support their arguments, and they know how to remain calm and confident throughout the negotiation. This is impressive—and it springs from assertiveness.

Before you can consider best practices and expand your skill set, you'll benefit from thinking through what being assertive really means. One way of understanding assertiveness is to think about the difference between knowledge and performance. You can't be assertive—you can't effectively ask for what you want—unless you first fully understand exactly *what* you want, *how* important this one goal is in relation to all your other goals, and *why* your desire is fair.

Perhaps you're looking to get more lab space, a modest request in line with what you imagine others in your department have. Consider this a green trail in skiing—a pretty easy negotiation. Maybe you want another assistant, which is certainly reasonable but a bit of a stretch compared to what you think your colleagues have on their teams. This is more like a blue square, intermediate trail.

Your request makes this slope steeper, and the response could be a mogul or two to overcome. Or maybe you want more space, more help, *and* more autonomy. This request could make this negotiation like a black-diamond expert trail. You'll need to be prepared for a steep, ungroomed hill with little room to maneuver and some hazards along the way.

If you want to get what you're asking for, once you have looked thoughtfully at your goal, you'll need to think about your performance. How can you ski the trail you've chosen? How can you best ask for what you want? Think about when you've been on the receiving end of a request. If someone is confident, patient, and tells a persuasive story, aren't you much more inclined to say yes?[14]

Remember that assertiveness can be a loaded term, sometimes tinged with criticism, particularly toward women and minorities who have been seen by some as too pushy or uppity. In the context of negotiation, however, assertiveness is not being aggressive, negative, or threatening. It is *not* pounding the table or raising your voice. Nor is it sulking or pretending to agree—and later sabotaging whatever was agreed on. It is not passive-aggressive behavior. Bullies do sometimes get their way, but over the long run, in an arena where reputation is crucial, bullying is not a recipe for long-term success.[15] Walking that line—firmly and pleasantly asking for what you want, holding onto your goals and trading off graciously, explaining why what you want is fair—is a skill that can lead to a lifetime of success.[16] And for most of us, it also takes a lifetime of practice.

To gauge your own general level of assertiveness, look at the following measurement tool. Please note that all of the tools in the book are just general places to start your self-analysis. Don't overthink an answer—your best bet is your first, gut response.

Assertiveness Scale

Read each item carefully and choose the appropriate number to indicate how well each item describes you. *What the Test Means & How to Score It: page 161*

Not at all like me	Somewhat like me	Fairly much like me	Very much like me

1. Most people seem to be more aggressive and assertive than I am.

4	3	2	1

2. When the food served at a restaurant is not cooked to my satisfaction, I complain to the person serving it.

1	2	3	4

3. I am careful to avoid hurting other people's feelings, even when I feel hurt myself.

4	3	2	1

4. If a well-known and respected lecturer makes a comment that I think is incorrect, I will have the audience hear my point of view as well.

1	2	3	4

5. I enjoy starting conversations with new acquaintances and strangers.

1	2	3	4

6. To be honest, people often take advantage of me.

4	3	2	1

7. If a close and respected relative upset me, I would hide my feelings rather than say I was upset.

4	3	2	1

8. I have sometimes avoided asking questions for fear of sounding stupid.

4	3	2	1

Not at all like me	Somewhat like me	Fairly much like me	Very much like me

9. I don't argue over prices with people selling things.

4	3	2	1

10. I tend not to show my feelings rather than upset others.

4	3	2	1

11. If a couple near me in a theater or at a lecture was conversing loudly, I would ask them to be quiet or take their conversation elsewhere.

4	3	2	1

12. Anyone attempting to push ahead of me in a line is in for a good battle.

4	3	2	1

13. I am open and honest about my feelings.

4	3	2	1

14. When I do something important or good, I try to let others know about it.

1	2	3	4

15. I am quick to express an opinion.

1	2	3	4

16. I do not like making phone calls to businesses or companies.

4	3	2	1

Now you're ready to look at how assertiveness works in negotiation—and minimal, average, and best practices. For each level, we offer advice for both preparation (the knowledge part of assertiveness) and performance (the actual ask). Every individual is usually better at one part of this than the other; bringing both elements together will help you be much more effective.

 When facing a green circle, a situation in which someone is likely to give you what you want (or one in which you really don't care that much about the outcome), you will need a minimal level of assertiveness preparation. This requires some level of knowledge about your own position in terms of what you want and why that is fair. For example, if you are seeking more lab space, before you walk into your chair's office to make your request, think about exactly what you need and why you need it. What will you accomplish with more space? Why will that accomplishment matter? You should think about your alternatives to an agreement. If the chair says no, what will you do? Share space with someone else? Not do the research? Leave? At the same time, you should set some goal for yourself in the negotiation. What would you specifically like to accomplish? (Chapter 13, about when you get your first grant, digs deeper into this type of scenario.)

Begin by setting some goals, the kind discussed in Chapter 3—goals that are specific, reasonable, and aspirational. Think about exactly what you want to get out of the negotiation, find words and phrases that accurately describe what you need, and detail why your request is reasonable.

On a green-circle trail, minimal practices in assertive performance include not negotiating against yourself. With or without knowing it, many of us can be our own enemy in negotiations, especially ones in which much is at stake, rushing through our own statements, anticipating (rather than listening to) the other person's response, interrupting others, or reacting too hastily to what's said or done during the meeting.[17] Think about this in advance and remember to listen and take things slowly: at the very least, wait for the other side to respond to your request verbally or in writing. Do not let his or her flinch, frown, or hesitation cause you to back away from your request too soon. Similarly, having thought about your alternatives, be firm when skating close to them. You do not want to end up worse off after the conversation than you were before it, so you don't want to get carried away by emotion and say something you haven't thought through. Before you get into the room, you'll need to decide your "bottom line"—the point at which you'll walk away from the negotiation.[18]

 For blue-square-trail negotiations, those that pose more challenges, you must use assertiveness during both the preparation and the actual performance. Add several elements to the level that you needed for green circles. Before you even think about how you will make your request, you should have fully researched the situation for yourself and other similar situations. Again, using the adding-lab-space-and-staff scenario, find out how much space and staff other comparable researchers in your department and other departments in the university have. Learn how others before you have been able to get more space and more help. In this research, take advantage of your contacts at other universities—what is the standard in your area of research at peer institutions? At your career stage? Once you have done this research, with information to back up why your goal is reasonable, you can set a realistic goal for yourself.

Then, in terms of negotiating strategy, think about your opening offer. Since most people expect every negotiation to have some give-and-take, don't ask for your ultimate goal at the start—you must aim reasonably higher than that and give yourself some room to bargain. Have an optimistic and fair opening offer and think about what your successive offers will be as the other side starts to negotiate.[19]

Think about the agenda of the overall negotiation—what issues need to be discussed and in what order. Remember that talking is not the only way to be assertive; asking questions and gathering information can serve you well as you fill out your knowledge about the situation.

While negotiating, the greater level of assertiveness needed for blue-square trails will focus on clearly communicating your position. Make eye contact, have confident and relaxed body language (open hands, relaxed seating), and make a clear ask. Wait for the other side to respond to your request. Having prepared a persuasive version of your story, deliver this story as a coherent whole.[20] When faced with questions, welcome them as an opportunity to further persuade rather than reacting defensively.[21]

 The practices in assertiveness needed for black-diamond negotiations (those in which you really care about your interests and perhaps are concerned about whether your counterpart will even listen to you), take top-notch preparation and top-notch performance. The good news on preparation is that this is a matter of persistence, research, and time. You don't have to change your personality or try to be someone you are not—you simply need to be knowledgeable about your own situation. And if what you want is a priority for you, isn't it worth your time to be well prepared? Remember: careful and thorough preparation will help you feel more confident and relaxed, which then will help your performance.

So how do you prepare? First, review what you know about the situation. How have other departments handled this situation? How has this person handled similar requests or situations? In other words, what might the other person view as precedent or fair? (The chapter on empathy will offer more about how to understand the other side's perspective.) Think about the other person's alternatives to reaching an agreement with you—how badly does he or she need you or your agreement? How replaceable are you? What would happen to the project if you were not on board with it? How important is it to the department that you are happy? To the chair?

Now review your own choices. Depending on how important this particular request is, if you do not get what you want, is there a point at which you would start to look for another job? Are there other alternatives to reaching an agreement? When would you start to pursue those? Reviewing all your possible alternatives—even when (and maybe especially when) they are not necessarily appealing—is crucial to understanding your choices.[22] After your review, choose your favorite alternative. What path are you most likely to pursue if you do not reach agreement? Will you accept the other side's offer but begin the process of looking for another job next year? Will you find a different project? In negotiation circles, this Best Alternative To a Negotiated Agreement is known as a BATNA.[23] And the point at which you would walk away to pursue that alternative is called your reservation point, your walk-away point, or your bottom line.

Then look at your priorities. Organizing them—deciding what is essential, optimal, or desirable—is not only helpful but important. And then think about whether any of your goals might be goals that the other side shares or would sign onto—getting a grant, for example, would benefit both you and your institution. It makes sense to start where you are both in agreement. Once your research is complete, identify your goals and organize your priorities, including your BATNA and your bottom line.

Finally, map out a strategy of your opening offer and what the next offer sequence could be. Think about what information you will share immediately and what information you would share only in exchange for gathering some information from the other person or other side.[24] Similarly, think about the other side's probable strongest arguments against what you want. What is the worst question your chair could ask you about your request for more space, more staff, and more autonomy? Prepare your response and counterarguments. All these strategies focus on understanding the "dance" of negotiation and using your preparation time to think about each dance step you will take. This way, even if your chair puts that "worst" question to you, if you have already considered the question and prepared an answer, you will not be thrown.

Now you are ready to implement black-diamond practices in performing assertively. Be sure to demonstrate confidence. Speak clearly, using short explanatory sentences as often as possible. Try not to hesitate, use "um," or end your sentence with a rise in your voice, as each of these common communication mistakes conveys a lack of confidence.[25] One well-known TED talk suggests practicing body language in advance—assuming a "power" position before you walk into the room so that you actually feel more confident when you speak.[26] Another strategy to build confidence is to stand on a chair to practice your statements and get used to projecting your voice.

Another best practice is to use questions to gather the information you need. Start with open-ended questions and then, if necessary or if the answer is not on point, ask more follow-up questions to get more information. Asking the same question with different words is a great way to be sure that you have all the relevant information. A frame of curiosity (discussed in the chapter on empathy) will help keep the tone of questions open, rather than judgmental.[27]

As you start to make your arguments, frame your story in the most persuasive light. Why will your idea help the chair, the other person, or the entire department? Why is your proposal fair? Best practices mean that you are also helping the other person sell your ideas to other decision-makers who might be involved. Think about how your chair might need to sell his or her own decision— why will you receive lab space when others have not, for example? Continue to think about the agenda and in what order you will cover your issues. Contemplate starting small to get the ball rolling.

Finally, as you ask for what you want, smile, take a deep breath, and ask. Then stop talking, so the other person is able to answer. You have already done the hardest thing: asking for what you want. Remember that even if your request is not granted, you have already demonstrated your professionalism in protecting your interests and pursuing your goals. Consider the fact that "no" can mean "not now." As facts and situations evolve, you can always ask again. Most negotiations at work are not "one-off" conversations but rather pieces of an ongoing relationship and multiple conversations. You may need to reopen a new set of issues at a later point, and that negotiation may lead to different set of outcomes.

Worse things could happen: You may have to take the lift up the mountain again and ski back down. But next time, you will be ready.

perceptions
UNDERSTANDING
perspective

CHAPTER 5
Empathy

Putting this in very simple terms, when you are negotiating, you are trying to change someone's mind. Empathy helps you figure out what the other person is thinking, and that insight into his or her mind can greatly improve your chances of changing it. Think of the other person's interests, positions, and wishes as the map of the territory you are trying to navigate:[28] When you understand what the other side thinks—and why he or she thinks it—you can start factoring that into your journey to reaching your own goals.

If you take time to consider the other person's (or the other side's) perspective, you will be more likely to be able to frame arguments in the way that will be persuasive to him or her. And empathizing with someone makes it more likely that he or she will empathize—or at least listen—to you. Finally, empathy helps build relationships through trust and respect. With that improved relationship, you will get more information and better, lasting outcomes.

Empathy has long been considered crucial to relationships.[29] Almost every culture has a saying about empathy. In Russia, people note that everyone views the world from his or her own bell tower. In the novel *To Kill a Mockingbird*, Atticus Finch tried to explain it to his daughter. You never really understand someone, he told Scout, until "you climb into his skin and walk around in it."[30]

What does empathy mean? Webster's defines it as "the action of understanding, being aware of, being sensitive to, and vicariously experiencing the feelings, thoughts, and experience of another of either the past or present without having the feelings, thoughts, and experience fully communicated in an objectively explicit manner." So it is the real understanding of the other side's perspective—why he or she thinks a certain way, and how that makes him or her feel.

Empathy is *not* sympathy or agreement, and therein lies the challenge. To accomplish your goal, you want to understand where the other person you're negotiating with is coming from—*and* at the same time still recognize the importance of your own interests. Some negotiators have difficulty continuing to think of their own view as "right" when they are working hard to understand the perspective of the other party, but the most successful negotiators manage this balance, recognizing that effective empathy gives them the ability to be more persuasive in asserting their own perspective and also makes it more likely that the other side will respond well to their assertiveness. If you understand what really matters to your chair, your colleague, or anyone else sitting across the table or the desk, you will be better able to persuade that person on his or her own terms.

True empathy consists of both cognitive and emotional understanding—understanding both *what* the other's person perspective is and *how* that perspective makes that person feel. Effective negotiators can build skills in both these arenas to improve their empathy. As with assertiveness, before you spend time investigating how to build these skills, see how you measure on this scale.

Empathy Scale

Read each item carefully and choose the appropriate number to indicate how well each item describes you. *What the Test Means & How to Score It: page 163*

Not at all like me	Not very much like me	Somewhat like me	Fairly much like me	Very much like me

1. When interacting with others, I often think about how I would feel if I were in the other person's position.

1	2	3	4	5

2. I feel as if I am sensitive to the feelings of others.

1	2	3	4	5

3. When I am upset with someone, I try to "put myself in his or her shoes."

1	2	3	4	5

4. I know that there are two sides to every issue, and I try to look at both sides.

1	2	3	4	5

5. I am often emotionally affected by things happening around me.

1	2	3	4	5

6. I sometimes don't feel much pity when I see someone being treated unfairly.

5	4	3	2	1

7. When I think I'm right about something, I don't spend much time listening to other people's arguments.

5	4	3	2	1

8. The misfortunes of others don't disturb me a great deal.

5	4	3	2	1

	Not at all like me	Not very much like me	Somewhat like me	Fairly much like me	Very much like me

9. I try to understand my friends better by imagining how a situation looks from their perspective.

1	**2**	**3**	**4**	**5**

10. I feel protective toward people if I believe they are being taken advantage of.

1	**2**	**3**	**4**	**5**

11. Before making a decision, I try to look at everyone's side of an issue.

1	**2**	**3**	**4**	**5**

12. Sometimes I don't feel sorry for people who are having problems.

5	**4**	**3**	**2**	**1**

13. I sometimes find it difficult to see things from another person's point of view.

5	**4**	**3**	**2**	**1**

14. I often feel concerned and sympathetic about people less fortunate than me.

5	**4**	**3**	**2**	**1**

Once you've answered the questions and scored your responses, you can turn to using both the cognitive and emotional kinds of empathy in negotiation.

 When skiing down an easy, green-circle trail (perhaps a situation in which you already know the other person well and the stakes are low, or maybe you need to ask a faraway colleague for a favor or register a complaint with customer service about your phone) a minimal practice of empathy starts with some research and observation.

Even before you start the conversation, take a minute to think. What is your best prediction of what the other party, your counterpart, might say or how he or she views this situation? Assess the current situation through the other person's eyes and think about how the other person might feel about you or your interests. As you enter the conversation, ask questions that will allow the other person to tell his or her story. Watch your counterpart's body language and tone for clues about the emotions behind the situation. Think about his or her motives and needs in this situation.

 When facing a blue-square trail, one that will involve higher intensity negotiations with perhaps a few bumps along the way, you will need to work more to add skills at each stage. One example of a moderately difficult negotiation might be that discussion with your chair about getting more lab space and staff.

In advance, prepare both open-ended and more directed questions, inquiries that will allow you to gain a fuller understanding of the other person's situation. Contemplate how your previous dealing with this counterpart (or the counterpart's own history) might affect his or her view of this situation. Are there other elements of the other person's own background or experience that would be useful to add to this calculation? If the last time your chair gave extra lab space to a researcher that researcher left a year later, might the chair be hesitant to grant you extra space, no matter how highly she regards you and your work?

During the actual negotiation, continue to ask questions in an open-ended and curious manner. Try to listen actively, using both good questions and open, inquisitive body language. (Much has been written and studied about "active listening." In short, active listening requires that the listener fully concentrate on the other person and understand, respond, and then remember what is being said. This almost laser-like focus is difficult to pull off, but it does get easier with practice.)[31] Pay attention to your counterpart while minimizing your own distractions. If you are tempted to justify your actions or defend yourself, take notes rather than interrupting. You will have the opportunity to share your opinion and your explanations later. Work on empathic accuracy—how carefully can you study your counterpart's nonverbal cues and how correctly can you interpret what you see? If your chair turns to a pile of papers on the desk after several minutes, is this a signal that she thinks the conversation is taking too long—or is she perhaps just looking for a piece of paper directly connected to the topic? What kind of eye contact does she make? Try to avoid attributing any particular meaning, especially bad intentions, to the other parties' physical or emotional response; what, other than impatience, might make the chair scowl? Might she be having an especially difficult day? Or just have a headache? Ask questions to clarify.

 If you are looking down a black-diamond slope, seeing steep drops, twists, and turns, you'll need to prepare thoroughly and take your best active listening skills into the negotiation. In advance of the negotiation, prepare yourself to have an open mind and to remain curious about how the other person views the situation. Review his or her past experience with you and with this situation, to better predict how this person might view the encounter. Think about what clarifying questions you will want to ask. Also review your own assumptions about the situation and, as you would for less steep and less dangerous trails, prepare questions that will help illuminate whether your assumptions are correct. To double-check your assumptions and gather even more information about what might happen, talk to others who have had interactions with your counterpart.

During the negotiation, for best practices, you will simultaneously be working on maintaining a nonjudgmental approach while asking questions and actively listening. One writer likens having empathy for the other person's story to hearing good music: you should listen carefully and appreciate it.[32] To stay open to the story, you will also need to be aware of your own reactions and monitor them.

If defensiveness threatens to overwhelm you, take a break to acknowledge your own feelings to yourself and refocus your attention (perhaps thinking and then writing "I don't think I can listen now because I want to interrupt and correct her version of events.") Writing down your responses so you can look back at them later is one good way of freeing your brain during the negotiation. This will help you ask questions in the moment without worrying that you might then forget what you had planned to say and the arguments you carefully prepared. By recording your responses on paper, you will give them the attention they deserve—but also be able to listen to your counterpart, to fully see his or her perspective and rationale. Once again, good questions prepared in advance will serve you well when you want to explore this perspective more deeply.

To navigate the moguls at this stage, be sure to loop back and double-check your information, assumptions, or understanding. ("So," you might say, "do I have this right? "You would prefer that I delay my grant submission until the next cycle?") This helps you avoid any misunderstanding, lets the other person know you heard what she or he said, and allows you to get information throughout the negotiation, not just at the beginning. This increased understanding and potentially new information will also help you with your other skills; once you understand that this delay is important to your chair (and why), you'll be more likely to be able to sell your own ideas. And, when the time comes to start talking about solutions, all the information you've gained and all the insights you've had into your chair's interests will enable you to come up with creative solutions that meet both your needs and those of your chair.

Being attuned to your counterpart's emotional state during the conversation will also help alert you to any impending hazards in the trail. All of us learn early on when—and when not—to discuss things with our parents by trial and error and by observation (not, for example, when you can see that both parents are exhausted after a hard day of work). The same holds true of negotiation: you will be most effective in negotiation if you consider your counterpart's emotional state and can judge how open he or she is to discussion. Studies of moods in negotiation show that happier people tend to be more creative and integrative,[33] while those who are unhappy more often end up in competitive situations.[34] (How you can create better moods for negotiation is discussed in Chapter 7, on social intuition.) When you can listen to the other person's emotions and show that you understand the emotions and the person, you are more likely to build trust and improve the relationship.[35] ("I think I see that you might be a bit hesitant to grant this request. Is that correct?") An extra advantage of these kind of emotion questions is that they double-check your reading of the other person. Maybe you are right—or maybe you've misread her pursed lips and hesitant responses. Either way, by either reflecting the emotion accurately or correcting your misimpression, you have improved the negotiation.

Empathy can also be shown through body language. Watch your own body to be sure that you are making eye contact (which at least in US culture is a sign of attention and connection), nodding, and keeping your face open. Mirroring body language, as we will discuss in the chapter on social intuition, can also build rapport.

Demonstrating empathy isn't easy, and doing this well, with both cognitive and emotional understanding, is far from easy on any kind of trail or negotiation. At times, you might feel as if just sitting and listening to the other person, speaking only to check to make sure that your understanding of his story is correct, is not accomplishing much and certainly isn't advancing your own story. But consider: when you speak about something very important to you, don't you want to be heard and understood? Listening and comprehending will connect you to the other person and let you see things, including your own story and your own goals, through his or her eyes—which is what empathy is all about. In the end, this skill, understanding where the moguls are and where hazards might be hiding, will help you navigate all kinds of trails.

shifting styles
CREATIVITY
OUTCOMES

CHAPTER 6
Flexibility

If you want to become a skilled, successful negotiator, you will want to think about flexibility in two ways. First, effective negotiators are flexible in terms of *how* they approach a negotiation. They understand the various styles of engaging—competing, accommodating, avoiding, collaborating, and compromising- that were covered in Chapter 2 and know how to choose a style to suit the context and the counterpart. One style may not be enough: these negotiators also are alert to signs that they need to change negotiation styles over the course of the negotiation, as the situation evolves.

Effective negotiators are also flexible in *what* they are willing to receive or what goes into a settlement. While they know that they need to remain protective of their own interests and goals (to be assertive, as discussed in the previous chapter), they understand that they must also remain open about which outcome might meet their interests. Recognizing that you can get what you need and want, your interests, in a number of ways will actually improve your chances of success. This mindset is key to best practices—recognizing that some opportunities might even create new value and get you more than you thought was available.

Flexibility is the ability to adapt strategically during the negotiation process to achieve a desired outcome. By now you are probably noticing a pattern: to organize best practices under flexibility, you will first need to think about the preparation you will need to be flexible in both your negotiating style and the substance of the negotiation. Particularly when you are trying to be flexible about the outcome of the negotiation, thinking on your feet in the middle of a negotiation, you will be much better off if you have taken time in advance to think about different elements of the solution.

Note that flexibility does not mean giving in or compromising your key interests (just as empathizing did not mean giving in or giving up on your own priorities and interests). It does mean thinking about how those interests can be met—and if there is more than one way to do that. Once again, you will notice a pattern: before you start thinking about using flexibility in negotiation, take some time to measure this for yourself using the following tool.

Flexibility Scale

Read each item carefully and choose the appropriate number to indicate how well each item describes you. *What the Test Means & How to Score It: page 165*

Not at all like me	Not very much like me	Somewhat like me	Fairly much like me	Very much like me

1. Even when times are bad, I always keep in mind that circumstances will get better.

1	2	3	4	5

2. I often find change to be difficult and challenging.

5	4	3	2	1

3. I find change to be a good thing.

1	2	3	4	5

Not at all like me	Not very much like me	Somewhat like me	Fairly much like me	Very much like me

4. I can easily come up with unconventional ways to solve problems.

1	**2**	**3**	**4**	**5**

5. When I have trouble reaching a goal, I can readily think of a number of different solutions.

1	**2**	**3**	**4**	**5**

6. I am very open to change.

1	**2**	**3**	**4**	**5**

7. When comparing myself to others, I believe I am an open-minded person.

1	**2**	**3**	**4**	**5**

8. I feel that I am responsive to a variety of messages and ideas.

1	**2**	**3**	**4**	**5**

9. It is important to me that I learn from people with whom I interact.

1	**2**	**3**	**4**	**5**

10. There are always many possible solutions to difficult situations.

1	**2**	**3**	**4**	**5**

11. There are many different aspects to reality.

1	**2**	**3**	**4**	**5**

12. There is more than one way to accomplish a goal.

1	**2**	**3**	**4**	**5**

Now let's look at how both process flexibility and outcome flexibility are used in negotiation.

 For a relatively easy green trail, one where much flexibility might not be needed and you can ski straight down, you should at least have thought carefully about the context. What, exactly, are you negotiating about? Where are you negotiating it? How important is it to you? Have you thought about the other side and what his or her typical style of negotiation has been in the past? All this is important in choosing a negotiation style to fit a particular negotiation.

For green-circle slopes and negotiations, preparation would be that you have examined your priorities going into the negotiation, carefully enough that you have thought about trading them off over the course of the negotiation. You recognize that negotiation often means working with the other side to find something that makes sense for both of you. Finally, while maneuvering down the hill during the negotiation, you are able to identify simple compromises using either common interests[36] (perhaps you and your mentor both want to increase department funding, so perhaps your mentor will agree to give you more research time in exchange for your writing a grant proposal to support it) or different ones[37] (you want to travel to a conference; your coauthor has no interest in going).

 To successfully navigate a blue-square slope, you must use flexibility during all three stages of negotiation: preparation, process, and outcome. For this preparation, start thinking about some potential tradeoffs in advance based on your knowledge of your interests and the interests of other side. Think about what else might sweeten the deal for your or for them in advance. In other words, prepare to be proactive in your flexibility.

During the process of the negotiation, flexibility in style means increased awareness of how your approach is working as well as the overall tenor of the negotiation. When things are moving along, staying with your selected negotiation style might make sense. If, on the other hand, things are getting stuck or heated, a good negotiator might be able to take a step back and shift approaches, changing tone and style to be more effective in dealing with this counterpart during a difficult exchange.[38] As noted in Chapter 2, different negotiating styles can be more or less effective when dealing with the counterpart's style, and a reasonably flexible negotiator will keep this in mind throughout the negotiation. Sometimes, when a negotiation continues over several sessions or weeks (as many conversations do), a negotiator with an average level of flexibility will consider the merits of changing styles for the next session. This requires careful attention: during the negotiation process, you will have to monitor the tenor of the negotiation as well as how well your approach is working so that you can strategically shift your tone or style as needed.

Finally, the level of flexibility needed while skiing a blue-square trail to achieve a solution means that during the course of the negotiation, a negotiator can start to take advantage of new information provided by the other side, to think of different solutions or outcomes. This requires recognition that the other side could well (and probably does) have information you do not yet know. This also requires something especially optimistic and challenging: a belief that the other side could actually propose something that could benefit you, as opposed to suggesting only things that you would want to dismiss automatically[39] and instantly. In other words, when considering successful outcomes, be open. Unless you are dealing with someone whose only goal is to shut you down completely, the other party often can have creative, helpful, and effective ideas.

 When facing a black-diamond trail in negotiation, a knowledgeable and effective negotiator definitely needs to prepare in advance. Best practices in flexibility require creativity and persistence during all stages of negotiation.

First, in thinking about how to approach the negotiation, you should spend some time researching how the other side typically negotiates or what his or her reputation is when dealing with similar situations. Think carefully about different types of styles and behaviors, almost preparing in a "what if?" mode, so that you can adapt your style in response to the other person's. Several years back, Andrea realized that she had too many administrative and committee assignments, responsibilities that were each important but together were taking up time that should have been devoted to research and scholarship. Rather than asking her dean to pull her off a specific committee, she visited him, explained the problem, and asked for advice. Much to her delight, the dean was more generous than she expected, removing more than one administrative task from her plate. It was, she recalls, a great lesson in flexibility and in the importance of remembering that the other side in negotiation might just propose a perfect solution.

Second, preparing for these more challenging trails means that you consider different options through a variety of more rigorous methods. One way is to use an "atlas of approaches" to your problem.[40] This technique considers how different professions or disciplines might view your issue. For example, if you are requesting more lab space, you are almost certainly thinking about how a researcher might view this idea. But you could also look at it from the perspective of an architect, an engineer, or an economist. An architect might think about all spaces in the building, an engineer might consider the structural aspects of your lab requirements, and an economist might examine who uses the lab at each time during the week and for what purpose.

Still another way to enlist creative thinking is called the "six-hats technique." Using this,[41] you examine the problem through different-color hats: red represents emotion; white, the facts; yellow is the positive aspects of the situation; green is the future implications; black is critiques; and blue is the process. Again, a review of different thinking processes might reveal that your concern over lab space is really a process question and that you are really worried about how this decision is being made. Your chair might be most concerned with future implications and the budget. The post-doc with whom you work could be mostly nervous about getting the work done. Either of these approaches or any structured advanced thinking on creative options helps you prepare to have flexibility in the final elements of the deal. After this preparation, you can come to the table with more than one way or strategy to meet your needs.

Flexibility over the course of the negotiation is a continuous dance of how and what to say. Best practices mean that you are adept at picking up on cues— you can identify and respond to tactics that are more hardball. You can also identify when it would be easier to be more assertive and get your way. You are recognizing new information in the moment, as it is shared, to monitor your results, and you remain open to the possibility of shifting your style yet again.

Finally, to navigate these challenging trails, flexibility over the outcome of the negotiation involves building on your careful preparation. As you respond to new information, you can share your own as appropriate and build solutions that incorporate this new information. You can reframe different or opposing interests into options that might meet your interests.[42] You might say, for example, "If I understand correctly, you feel that summarizing our study results for the conference proposal is a hassle. What if I were to summarize the results? If so, would it be okay with you if I attended the conference either with you or for the both of us?"

You are persistent in thinking about how to address an issue rather than just splitting the difference at the first sign of resistance. During the negotiation, you can engage in creative techniques with your counterpart. Simple brainstorming is relatively easy; ask your counterpart why (or why not) or ask for critiques of your proposals. When faced with barriers—financial or otherwise—continue to ask questions.

Think of posing the "magic wand" or "Croesus" question, asking your counterpart what he[43] or she (or you two together) could do if one or both of you were the richest king in all of ancient Lydia, unlimited by time, money, talent, technology, or effort. When making your own proposals, think about proposing more than one option at a time. Instead of "would you accept this one plan?" ask which option—A, B, or C—would work best.[44] And, as noted above, be sure to remain open-minded to proposals, carefully considering how they might meet your interests or be the basis of something that could work for both of you. Think of flexibility—both in process and outcome—as the skill that helps you navigate any terrain. To get to the base of the mountain, you need to bend your knees, get ready to absorb a few bumps, and always be willing to maneuver.

BODY LANGUAGE
mirroring
eye contact

CHAPTER 7
Social Intuition

In negotiation, getting what you want from your counterpart has much to do with how she or he feels about you. Does she trust you? Like you? How can you communicate over the course of the negotiation in ways that will increase the likelihood of building rapport and trust? When you seek to affect the other person on both substantive and process-related levels, you must attend to the negotiation communication itself as well as the thinking patterns and attitudinal elements that surround it.

When people interact, they engage in exchanges of information on cognitive and subliminal levels. Some of this information relates to whatever they are substantively talking about. Other aspects of the information exchanged relate to each party's emotions—about themselves, about the substance of the conversation, and about the other party or parties.

These communication channels provide the building blocks for many of the intangible—yet solidly important—elements that affect and control interactional patterns, overall strategic approach, and actual decision-making. Issues such as trust, rapport, and power are all translated through this intuitive communication.

The degree to which one is adept at navigating this little-charted terrain is captured by the term social intuition.

To understand this phrase and consider its practical implementations in negotiation, think of it in three elements:

Self: This aspect might be best understood as self-awareness with regard to your own emotions, cognitive patterns, biases, attributions, and reactions. Studies have long shown that people with more self-control (those who are willing and able to delay gratification, for example) are more successful in academia.[45] This kind of self-control can show up as monitoring your emotional tenor during the negotiation, which then brings better control of how you come across. You can measure this part of social intuition by examining your tone, your pace of conversation, how you carry yourself physically in the negotiation (are you tense? are your shoulders elevated?), and even how your emotions show on your face.[46] Do your words (the content) match your conduct (the process)? When you smile to put someone at ease, does your smile go all the way to your eyes?[47] How you set the mood in a negotiation also comes into play here. So the first step in social intuition is the ability to be aware of your own emotional tenor.

Other: This aspect is essentially the ability to read your counterpart. Can you note and understand his signals in body language, nuance, attention span, laugh, volume, tone, and voice responses? Does her behavior seem consistent (or incongruent) with what she is saying substantively and what you understand to be her interests? In this aspect, you are working to stay attuned to the other person's emotional state and how it is reflected through conscious and unconscious signals.[48]

Bridging: This third aspect involves *action* you take to form connections with the other through the interactional exchange—connections that support you in *affecting* the other. How do you use this to focus your goals? Your actions, for example, the things you do to help the other person feel more at ease (or not)— fall under bridging. Actions under this aspect of social intuition include physical and tonal mirroring. When your department chairs leans forward, so do you. As she picks up the pace of conversation, you respond in kind. Bridging actions can fall under body language, space, pace of communication, tone, and humor and can include all sorts of little responses you might not even be aware of. Negotiation writers call bridging part of the "dance" of negotiation[49]—and when it works well, counterparts look and feel as if they are moving together, even when substantive differences remain. Your situational awareness—your ability to read yourself, read the other person, and read the situation—all come together.

This triad of capacities—being self-aware, reading others, and bridging—join together to form the essential negotiator attribute or skill we call social intuition. Social intuition is different from empathy, which is the cognitive understanding of what your counterpart is thinking and feeling. Social intuition is the ability to read yourself, read your counterparts, and manage *their* emotions, experiences, attributions, and responses through your own actions. As always, before you work on practicing and improving social intuition, it's helpful to find out where you stand now.

Social Intuition Scale

Read each item carefully and choose the appropriate number to indicate how well each item describes you. *What the Test Means & How to Score It: page 167*

True	False

---

1. When I'm talking with people, I often notice subtle social cues about their emotions–discomfort, say, or anger–before they acknowledge those feelings in themselves.

| 1 | 0 |

---

2. I often find myself noting facial expressions and body language.

| 1 | 0 |

---

3. I find it does not really matter whether I talk with people on the phone or in person because I rarely get any additional information from seeing someone I'm speaking with.

| 0 | 1 |

4. I often feel as if I know more about people's true feelings than they do themselves.

1   **0**

5. I am often taken by surprise when someone I'm talking with gets angry at something I said, for no apparent reason.

0   **1**

6. At a restaurant, I prefer to sit next to someone I'm speaking with so I don't have to see his or her full face.

0   **1**

7. I often find myself responding to another person's discomfort or distress on the basis of an intuitive feel rather than an explicit discussion.

1   **0**

8. When I am in public places with time to kill, I like to observe people around me.

1   **0**

9. I am uncomfortable when someone I barely know looks directly into my eyes during conversation.

0   **1**

10. I can often tell when something is bothering another person just by looking at him or her.

1   **0**

To understand how social intuition works in negotiation, think about how it looks in different situations and at different skill levels.

 In a simple, green-circle, easy negotiation with minimal stress between the parties, social intuition means being aware of how you are feeling and what emotions you are likely to have in the conflict or negotiation. Then, during the negotiation, you are able to manage your behavior. Perhaps you do not reveal exactly how frustrated you are. Similarly, you are also able to hide your delight if the initial offer is excellent, and you continue to negotiate rather than accept the first offer. You are aware of your own body language and mannerisms and how others might read them. (For example, if you cross your arms, one tucked into the other across your chest, because the room is cold, you know that others might interpret this posture as meaning you're closed off, not open to new ideas, so you will make a comment about the room's chilly temperature or rub your hands along your forearms to make sure your body language is not misread.)

Social intuition when dealing with others in these low-stress encounters means that you start to be attuned to their emotions and reactions during the negotiation. You recognize that being in an argument with someone does not necessarily mean you should be argumentative. You might temporarily avoid certain subjects until later in the conversation, for example. You use body language and actions like maintaining eye contact or nodding to show respect to your counterpart and encourage his or her continued participation in the conversation.[50]

 For blue-square trails and intermediate challenges, you will need to build on your social intuition skills to manage your emotions effectively throughout the negotiation. You are aware of yourself, your emotional temperature, and how you are focusing. You might, for example, take a break to cool down or refocus if needed. You use body language effectively to convey positive and negative emotions in a purposeful, rather than reactive, manner (leaning in toward the other person,[51] sending a clear signal that you are interested in what she is saying).

When dealing with your counterpart on these more challenging trails, work on your ability to read a situation and understand what is socially appropriate and what your counterpart expects. Laugh (politely, if necessary) at his jokes, respond to his positive comments with positive responses, and make your own comments and jokes to put the other side at ease. Read the other person's body language and synchronize yours—leaning in, smiling, and using open hand gestures. Take notes and nod as the other person speaks, to convey that you are listening. Here, as with other skills, preparation will help you manage these sometimes-tricky slopes with comfort; if you have researched both the subject and the other person before the conversation begins, you'll already have thought about how you might build connections.

 For black-diamond trails, you will need to practice full self-attunement. You are self-aware; you are comfortable with your role in this negotiation and with your arguments. You convey the fact that you are comfortable though encouraging words, supportive body language, and other nonverbal cues. During the negotiation, you remain non-defensive and manage your natural self-interested inclinations, particularly as the conflict gets more heated.

When dealing with your counterpart in these black-diamond interactions, you need to use social intuition to show the outward signs and language of the kind of comfort you have worked hard to reach. You are curious and keep your language open-ended and nonjudgmental. Before the negotiation, you should research what you can find out about your counterpart, and you then can use this research to ask questions, find commonalities, and make the other person feel at ease. (If the office is decorated with a sports team banner, for example, you might mention that; if you see a giant fish hanging on the wall, you can ask about its origin.) You should also research potential cultural differences that might arise, though be careful not to make generalizations or fall into stereotypical thinking (not everyone from the East Coast, for example, speaks quickly).

During the actual negotiation, you are able to mirror or synchronize with your counterpart's verbal and body language, which keeps him or her comfortable. Your pace of speech, the length of a pause, and the tilt of your body all can mirror the other person's and help set a collaborative tone. You can think about the metaphor being used in the conversation, and perhaps use a different one to subtly change the tone. (Instead of more competitive metaphors stemming from war or sports, for example, you might use a more collaborative one from construction or dance.) When an impasse occurs, you do not get visually frustrated. You remain relaxed and work collaboratively. You demonstrate patience and self-restraint. When the situation escalates, you are able to reframe the issues, to help both you and the other party learn from them.

These very important social intuition skills are the glue that help builds trust and rapport during the negotiation. Often, without our even noticing, these moves are the ones that actually build a relationship and facilitate information exchange. Tracking your own awareness, reading your counterpart, and then responding effectively are all part of the negotiation dance that keep you from falling flat on your face.

Like the downhill skier who has bundled up for the fierce cold wind, has taken time to get to know the course and all the possible obstacles in it, and has carefully practiced experiencing and responding to each patch of ice or stretch of pure powder, you proceed down the mountain with skill and attention.

CHAPTER 8
Ethicality

Ethicality relates to the relationship between the parties during the negotiation and, equally important, affects the compliance and follow-through of any agreement that is reached. Effective negotiators will take both their own and their counterpart's level of ethicality into account before, during, and after the negotiation.

Think of ethicality in three ways: reputation, trustworthiness, and trustfulness. Your reputation is how others perceive you. It is connected to whether others can trust you, but it is not completely the same as trust because reputation encompasses more than trust. Furthermore, trust and distrust operate separately from each other—you might trust your chair to pursue the department's interests, for example, but distrust her to put her own interests aside while doing so.[52]

Reputation

The reputation of the negotiator is a crucial part of ethicality. In almost all the interactions within an academic or research setting, each time you negotiate, you will be operating from the foundation of your established reputation—and at the same time adding to or even remaking that reputation.

Think back to your previous dealings with counterparts. What has been your typical approach to dealing with your mentor, your chair, and your colleagues? What skills do you excel in, and what skills could you improve? How does your counterpart perceive you?

Negotiations are inherently uncertain, and a reputation helps manage this uncertainty by giving others signals or predicting how you will behave[53]—and why. The phrase "your reputation precedes you" is apt; just as you researched the person you were going to negotiate with, you should expect that the other person has done research on you, at the least asking around about what to expect from you in the coming meeting. Your reputation, then, will explain your actions and motivations in any interaction in which the other party does not fully know what other options or information you have. If you have a reputation for working well with others, for instance, your actions will be interpreted in that light—with that "halo" of a cooperative approach[54] influencing your current negotiation. If word has it that you often see the merits in compromising, your counterpart will be thinking about that during your meeting. As empirical negotiation studies have clearly demonstrated, different reputations can lead to different outcomes.[55]

Your counterpart's reputation can also affect the negotiation significantly. Not surprisingly, when a counterpart is known to be adversarial and have a competitive approach to negotiations, negotiators share less information, waste more time talking around the subject, and achieve less beneficial and creative outcomes.[56] Having a reputation for being competitive, of course, can be useful in certain situations, especially when you are trying to deter someone from even beginning to negotiate with you or when you are making threats and want the other side to believe you will carry them out.[57] In the majority of scenarios described in this book, however, these interactions will benefit from a long-term perspective that seeks to bring together multiple interests.

When parties have the reputation for being integrative or problem-solving, the result is likely to be more satisfying.[58] Facing someone with a good reputation makes people more inclined to share information and to share it more efficiently and earlier in the negotiation, which saves time. This increased information-sharing then leads to better, more comprehensive agreements. For example, in a study examining lawyers negotiating with each another, lawyers who had negotiated with each other before were more apt to reach agreement than those who had never done business together—even if their first meeting had not ended in agreement.[59] Think about the reputation of those you respect—colleagues, family, or friends—and note what type of skills these individuals typically use.

You will also want to consider your reputation moving forward. Particularly if many of your negotiations will be repeat interactions, occurring with the same parties over and over again (your mentors, your coauthors, your chair), looking ahead is essential to your long-term success. Consider how you start a negotiation. Setting a good tone, schmoozing, and communicating are crucial in creating a reputation (and are also tied closely to social intuition). These skills are not only important for what they accomplish during a negotiation but how they then contribute to or create your reputation, which affects future encounters. Consider, too, how you end a negotiation. When things go your way, be sure not to gloat. When you are not happy about the result, maintain a professional demeanor (so that you can negotiate again?). In the long run, petulance will not help.

When reflecting on your own actions and how they create your reputation, look at them from a variety of perspectives. Years from now, will you look back on your conduct and be proud or ashamed of it? If you were the hero in a novel,[60] how would the author describe your actions and reactions? Was your behavior impressive enough that it might contribute to some sort of good policy that your institution might adopt? If one of your parents had behaved as you did, what would you think? If an account of your behavior appeared tomorrow on the front page of *The New York Times* or on Facebook, would you be embarrassed?

As we move through life, many of us keep in mind an emotional advisor or someone we want to influence. Perhaps your grandmother is your moral anchor. Perhaps you want to make sure you set a good example for your children. Whatever their reference is, effective negotiators understand that their behavior continually creates a reputation over time, one that can help or harm them in the next negotiation.

This theme will thread through the scenarios that make up the latter part of this book. In short, you never know who will be where five years from now or what collaborative work might be possible, so keeping your name clean is crucial. In Chapter 14, when Zoe is negotiating with Madeleine about a possible coauthored chapter, she should be aware of Madeleine's reputation as well as understanding that in this dynamic Zoe is creating her own. When Zach, in Chapter 18, is weighing his options for promotion, looking at offers from a Midwestern university, an Ivy League school, and the college where he now works, he should remember that each interaction adds to his reputation. Even if he does not pursue the Ivy League offer, his meetings there will define him, create his reputation, among the people at that university. And when he leaves his current workplace, he will want to depart graciously.

Trust

Trust is one other key component of your reputation, and it is so important to creating your reputation over time, particularly in ethicality, that it merits its own discussion.

As noted earlier, trust and distrust are distinct, and they can and often do coexist regarding the same person. You might trust someone to perform research—but not trust him to write it up in the careful, professional way that you require. You might trust your mentor to help you get a paper published—but not to help you leave her lab when the time is right for you to move on.

As you negotiate with your mentor, which is discussed in Chapter 11, keep this complexity in mind. Rather than thinking of trust and distrust as opposite ends of one spectrum, think of them as separate spectrums that coexist in each situation. With that distinction in mind, consider two key concepts under ethicality that both involve trust.

Trustworthiness

The first is the idea of trustworthiness. In negotiation, trustworthiness means that the other side can take you at your word. This trust comes because you have consistently performed as you said you would. Trustworthiness means that you will follow through on actions, that you will not mislead, and that you are dependable.

Trustworthiness can help negotiations in a variety of ways. When you trust someone, you are more likely to want to deal with him or her because you have confidence that he or she will be credible and follow through on commitments. This trust also will make the negotiation more efficient because the agreement itself will be shorter—two people who trust each other do not need spell out every single component of their resolution. They trust each other to abide by the agreement and to act in its spirit. (Imagine an agreement to coauthor in which you had to spell out all the elements of coauthoring—who will write what by what date with what parameters; who will edit what when; who will deal with the publisher. An agreement to mentor would be even more ludicrous if you had to outline every element.) Increased trust between the parties means that whatever the agreement is, the relationship will be strong and perhaps grow even stronger over the life of the agreement.

When trying to increase your level of trustworthiness in a relationship, consider a number of steps. While some of these may appear obvious or just common sense, listing them can still be helpful.

1   Perform competently. Show your ability to carry out duties and obligations.

2   Create and meet the other party's expectations. Establish consistency and predictability. Be clear about what you intend to do and then do what you said you would.

3   Stress the benefits of creating mutual trust. Point out the advantages for the other person, or for both of you, of maintaining such trust. Keep your promises.

4 Establish credibility. Make sure your statements are honest and accurate. Tell the truth, and keep your word. Communicate accurately, openly, and transparently.

5 Show concern for others. Act in a way that respects and protects other people. Show sensitivity to their needs, desires, and interests.

6 Share and delegate control where you have it. Share power and allow the other person to have voice and control over the process.

7 Develop a good reputation. Work to make others believe you are someone who has and deserves a reputation for being trusting and acting in a trustworthy manner.[61]

Trustfulness

Finally, consider the concept of trustfulness under the rubric of ethicality. Effective negotiators are able to trust the other side—at least somewhat—to get something done. Too much suspicion or hesitation about working with the other side can become a self-fulfilling prophecy in which, if you are suspicious of the other person, he or she should be suspicious of you.[62] On the other hand, trustfulness should not be naive or all-consuming. You do not need to believe everything.

Understandably, your willingness to be trustful of the other party will depend on his or her reputation and trustworthiness. For this reason, if you are going to sit down with someone you don't know (or don't know well), plan to invest time in advance researching the other person's reputation. Even when you have negotiated with the person before, at least take some time to think about his reputation. How does he generally act in such meetings? What is his typical way of dealing with conflict? What have you learned (or heard) about his negotiation style?

Similarly, you will want to examine your counterpart's level of trustworthiness. Would you trust your lab technician to finish a task that she promised to do? Would you trust the lead author on an article to put your name in the order promised? In other words, does the other person perform as she or he has pledged to?

For some matters, you will want to look for a deeper level of trust. Would you trust your mentor to negotiate with your chair on your behalf? Sometimes this level of trust is warranted—you know from experience that the other person is as committed to your interests as you are and has the skill set or position to be able to protect you. On the other hand, sometimes it is not.

Consider just one case of misplaced trust. Years ago, Tali, a promising scientist with a PhD in neuroscience who was finishing her medical specialty training in psychiatry, was negotiating for her first faculty position. She liked where she was working and wanted to stay on, and her mentor assured her that he would work directly with the department chair to make that happen. When things were not moving, she talked with the chair, who also assured her that she would receive a good package to get her started. (Note: Stories such as Tali's are all based on real examples but, to protect people's privacy, we have not used real names and have changed some details.)

Several months passed with no approach from Tali's university. Finally, at the end of the academic year, she received an offer to work at the university as an advanced research fellow with a salary that was lower than that of a faculty member, less starting funds than she had expected, and no ability to apply for independent funding. By that point, Tali knew she had no time to look elsewhere, so she accepted the position. Her great trust in her mentor and her chair blinded her to the harsh reality of the style of the players and the overall ethos of the institution. More research into their past behaviors and their reputations would have been wise. She vows she will not make that mistake again, but she knows she has lost valuable time.

To be effectively trustful (and not naïve), think about defenses against deception. What can you do to reduce the likelihood that others will try to bluff or lie to you?[63]

As always, and as Tali learned, research is a great start. Network with others in your field to find more information about your counterpart's reputation. During the negotiation, remembering the importance of social intuition, create rapport by employing your best social and conversational skills. When your counterpart feels at ease with you, she or he will probably be less likely to deceive you,[64] and your own sense of trustfulness will increase as well.

Then during the actual negotiation, go back to the objective standards that you researched to be assertive. When the agreement is based on those fair standards, you—and the other person—will be able to have more trust in the outcome.

As a third step, be strategic and careful in sharing information. Trust can be very helpful in moving negotiations forward, but you want to share information in a way that protects you. Make sure that the other side is also sharing information: for each piece of information he or she offers, be sure to ask questions and gather information. At the end of this information exchange,[65] and particularly in new situations, returning to broad questions can also be helpful. For example, "Is there anything else I should know about the department before accepting an offer?"

And, as you start to interact based on an agreement, note your counterpart's behavior. Is it what you expected? Observing her or his performance will help prepare you for the next negotiation. Do you need to be more specific in the next agreement? Did the chair take advantage of you this time (so next time you need to be more on guard)? Know your counterpart's reputation and keep your long-term game plan in mind.

Despite your best intentions, sometimes you will violate the trust of others. Here is some advice for rebuilding your reputation.

Take action immediately after the violation. Do not let the violation of trust linger, and do not make your counterpart have to confront you about the violation. Second, apologize to your counterpart and thoroughly explain what happened. Sincerely express remorse and also detail why the violation occurred so that your counterpart can understand your thinking. Third, provide penance of some kind, an appropriate compensation. And finally, restate or renegotiate expectations for the future—and then be sure to live up to them. You will probably be "on probation" for some time, so you need to reestablish trust.

What you have probably gathered from the discussion of reputation, trustworthiness, and trustfulness is that all three work together—under the rubric of ethicality—to serve as crucial threads for your relationships and your negotiations. If any one of these is suspect, the fabric will fall apart. Each concept is linked to each other, to you, and to your counterpart.

Negotiation effectiveness requires that you be constantly cognizant of your own reputation, your own trustworthiness, and your own willingness to trust. At the same time, you should be critically examining all three elements of your counterpart's ethicality and adjusting your behavior accordingly.

differences
STRATEGIES
defaults
modes

CHAPTER 9
Communication Choices

With today's technology, we have many choices about how to communicate, and negotiations are often played out over one or more of these modes. Because each communication method has its own distinct advantages and challenges, however, you should choose which one you use with care and purpose.

As anyone with a smart phone and a social media profile knows, you can manage your communication in a variety of ways. Today we call, we email, we text, we post on Facebook (and Facebook message), we Snapchat, we Skype, we Instagram, we tweet, and, within a few years, we will probably communicate in some way we haven't even thought of today. Many of these modes seem to operate seamlessly: in making plans for dinner with friends, you might have emailed to set the date, called on the phone to debate the pros and cons of various dining options, and texted to let your companions know you were running late. Your dinner conversation is then face-to-face.

In a professional relationship, these choices are more nuanced. When do you stop by your colleague's office for a chat? When do you call to talk to your chair about some differences in your approach? And when you are communicating in writing, when do you email and when do you text? When and how should you actually write a letter?

Differences in Modes of Communication

Once again, stepping back—this time to examine the differences between various communication modes and think about how they operate in a negotiation— is useful.

As researchers have noted, face-to-face conversations are considered media "rich" because they allow tracking of multiple social cues.[66] In face-to-face conversations (in person and online via video), you can see and interpret body language, tone, eye contact, and facial expressions as well as the audio content. Phone conversations provide some of this; by listening to the tone, pauses, and inflections of spoken conversation, you can learn a lot about how the other party is feeling. Emails or texts, on the other hand, do not incorporate those contextual elements, although you can add "e-empathy" to your email and text communication, to try to bring in that media richness.

The difference between modes of communication is also reflected in the content that comes across. In face-to-face conversations, the conversation often rapidly switches between the personal and the professional, the blandly general (think the weather) and the intensely personal. In email communications, content tends to be more task-oriented.[67] What needs to get done? What is the answer to this question? Unless you take a little extra time to add personal touches (often at the beginning or end, or both), an email is usually less personal than direct conversation. In US culture, most of us have been trained to start off a face-to-face conversation or negotiation with at least some small talk or pleasantries. This same impulse does not necessarily occur online.

Timing is another noticeable difference. Face-to-face conversations are, by their very nature, synchronous conversations. In other words, both parties are engaged at the same time. Even when one side is talking, the other person is interacting through body language and responses. Online communication may occur simultaneously, particularly with texting, but only if both parties happen to be on their devices at the same time and if they choose to engage that way.

Chances are you often send emails without knowing whether the recipient will read them immediately—or even anytime soon. Emails can and do stack up: you've probably had the experience of sitting down at your computer, phone, or tablet and finding 10 emails in your inbox in reverse chronological order, and in poring through them discovering that a crisis or question, posed with great urgency several hours ago, has since been resolved.

Surely you have also experienced the seeping of email communication into nonwork hours; the asynchronicity of these communications means that although your "work" hours might be over, your work emails can continue (for better and worse) throughout your waking and nonwaking hours. This flexibility—and the fact that you can receive emails and texts on mobile devices and even on your wristwatch when you're dining, watching television, or putting your kids to bed—can make emails and texts both distracting and hard to digest. There are other drawbacks to mobile communication: reading long, complicated emails on a small smartphone isn't always easy, and doing so late into the night can strain your sleep as well as your eyes. Notably, many of us also tend to read emails from most recent to last recent, meaning that we read them in the opposite order in which they were generated.

Why Differences Matter in Negotiation

As discussed earlier, trust and relationships are important factors in negotiation. Much of your ability to create rapport comes from your ability to see—or at least hear—the other person, but in emails, body-language mirroring skills, eye contact, and even small gestures such as a nod are all useless, so when you send and receive email messages, you will have much less context for the content. When a colleague says she was crushed not to receive a draft of the chapter today, is she joking? How about a boss's disappointment that you missed a meeting? In face-to-face communication, you are almost always able to tell immediately whether the speaker is sad or happy, joking or snarky. But with email, you have to guess. Especially in work situations and more formal contexts or when dealing with superiors, all of us tend to read emails more analytically and literally, since the words are the only information we have. In short, in interpreting email messages, we are more likely to assume bad intentions or worry that something is wrong than we would if the same words were expressed in person.[68]

The content of the information exchange in email is also different. Without the ability to explain, ask questions, and clarify ambiguities in real time, it's easy to make assumptions about the content of an email. Even when you ask questions, they might not be answered directly—or the response might address only one of the two questions you posed in the email.

Developing relationships and trust through email is more challenging than in person. Several studies have shown that when they negotiate, parties are more adversarial with each other via email (and even over the phone) compared to face-to-face meetings.[69] Parties tend to share less information and cooperate less in the process of negotiation via email, resulting in lower levels of trust and higher potential for deceptive practices.[70] And without the facial and verbal cues of face-to-face communication, people tend to have higher levels of negative attribution. In other words, they assume the worst and are more likely to attribute poor motives to their counterpart.

How Differences Matter in Negotiation

These differences all play out in negotiation, where each form of communication can help—or hurt. There is no one "right" way to communicate during negotiation, and in today's busy workplaces, many negotiations use more than one mode. You just need to think carefully about the pros and cons of each throughout the course of the negotiation, being mindful of which mode of communication might work best in any one particular context at any one particular time.

If cooperating is your goal, for instance, email is not going to make that easy. With less information exchanged and more opportunity for distrust, integrative solutions are harder. But because email does allow parties to outline their thoughts in writing more fully than they might have in person, an extended email negotiation can create opportunities for logrolling and trade-offs.

Another plus: in an antagonistic relationship or when dealing with a difficult topic, one you might be hesitant about raising, the distance email provides might actually help, moving things forward without emotion clouding your argument. Email can also be better in reducing unconscious bias and permitting more participation by "lower-status" people.[71] In a face-to-face group setting, senior leaders typically dominate the conversation, and once they have made their views clear, other participants tend to go along. But in a free-flowing email conversation that has already started, lower-status people participate more. Once one person expresses doubts, others feel freer to chime in with their concerns.

Understanding Your Defaults

As you contemplate how to choose modes of communication, examine yourself and your counterpart in terms of default modes. Ask yourself a simple question. When you pull out your phone, what is the first app that you check? Do you look at your incoming calls? Your text messages? Your email? Facebook or other social media? This is your default—at least with your personal communications—and the mode of communication with which you are most comfortable.

Perhaps more important than your comfort level is your skill level at each of these modes. Examine all the modes to think about your strengths and weaknesses. Do you prefer to make requests in person or via email? When you have a question for a colleague, do you email him or her or pick up the phone? One approach is to communicate through your most comfortable mode, as long as that mode seems acceptable to the other party, because it will help you ask for what you want.

Understanding Their Defaults

At the same time, of course, you need to learn about the modes of communication your counterpart prefers to negotiate in. This does not mean that you always choose that particular mode—rather that you have consciously thought about the choice. So first think about the other person's habits when communicating with you. Does she show a preference for email, phone, videoconference, or face-to-face conversations? How technologically savvy is your counterpart? Some of us will deal with colleagues who are early adopters—they were tweeting before you even heard of Twitter, and they have been wearing an Apple watch since the day it came out. Other colleagues are more traditional, so phone calls will be necessary to draw their attention to the email that you sent. The point here is not to judge but to understand what method will be most persuasive. Sometimes this is contextual—someone might regularly text his children but tend toward email for professional communications. And sometimes it is generational, so that someone is most comfortable with the form of technology she first started using when it was new, whether that means phoning, emailing, or texting. In a professional context, the initial communication may be the most formal—you might, for instance, want to send an email with a letter attached, but that might not prove to be the best mode for the actual negotiation.

As the relationship evolves, as many work relationships do, staying attuned to modes—and tones—of communication will be helpful. As you get to know your chair or your mentor, both your relationship and the tone and form of your communication will probably reflect this increased ease: perhaps your emails have a more casual tone, or maybe you start texting short notes. A counterpart may, over time, get used to a new device, one he avoided in the past, and become comfortable using it. Technology and social media themselves will change, allowing different, new modes of communication. Skype and FaceTime, which today are so helpful in allowing face-to-face connections for phone calls (and all the rapport that makes possible) and so commonplace that their names have become verbs, did not even exist 20 years ago.

Thinking Strategically about How to Communicate

Once you have thought about your defaults and those of your counterpart, consider a few more elements. Timing, as the saying goes, is everything, so you will want to keep that aspect of communication tools in mind. If you can reach someone on the phone or in his or her office, for example, your communication will be immediate, so if you need a quick answer, the phone might be your first choice. On the other hand, people are often slower in returning phone messages than they are emails or texts (which is another factor to consider in thinking about your counterpart's defaults). Which mode is likely to get the quickest response?

These considerations could mean you choose a series of communications. You might, for example, stop by someone's office and then follow up with an email if he or she is not there. Or you might send a long email explaining a complicated issue but leave a quick voicemail (or text) letting the person know that a more detailed email is awaiting her response.

Other times, if your goal or purpose is different, you could shift the sequence of your modes of communication. You might use one form of communication for record-keeping (email is particularly good for this), and another for prompting a response. After an in-person meeting, you might want to record the details of the exchange in an email that you send to the other person, just to confirm your understandings of the conversation. Consider Skyping or calling before you send that complicated request by email; studies show that even a short phone call in advance of a longer email helps break the ice and build rapport.[72]

Finally, you should always be thinking about the importance of the communication. A short text or phone call letting someone know you are running late is perfectly appropriate. But at least today, your chair probably would consider a text asking for a raise to be unprofessional. For significant interactions, professional exchanges should probably still be via letter—even if the "letter" is a pdf that you send via email.

Skills in Modes of Communication (Particularly Online)

Negotiation guidelines (be assertive, empathetic, flexible, and socially intuitive) often assume that the interaction is in person, but the skills they list are just as important when you are using other modes of communication. You just have to think of the skills in different terms.

For assertiveness via email, for example, your prose needs to be well constructed. An email that is riddled with misspellings, missing words, and incomplete sentences probably will not be taken seriously and will certainly undercut your message, so if grammar and spelling are not your strong suits, take extra time to review your emails before you send them. If your word processing program has a spell-check function, use it. Make sure your language is clear—and use the subject line of the email to help your counterpart understand what you are talking about. Be sure to outline and frame your requests as persuasively as you would in person. And beware of putting too much in an email—particularly when they are reading emails on their phones, people often do not make it all the way to the end of a very long email.[73] Instead, you might want to create a short email, write a longer letter or document, and attach the document to the email (and hope the other person will take time to download and read the attachment) or send separate emails for separate requests. But be careful to track all your email correspondence; you do not want to miss or lose a response to a pressing question.

Keeping in mind that you can sometimes be both creative and flexible in emails, use those communications to clearly outline options: "I could work on this project or I could research another avenue" might get a better response from the other party once he or she has had some time to reflect on your options. Similarly, reading emails to understand the other person's priorities—and having the ability to reread and reflect—might help you generate options. On the other hand, if talking is your way of thinking something through, video conferencing or conversing face-to-face makes more sense.

Creating and demonstrating empathy in emails is a recognized challenge. Emojis, smiley faces, and exclamation points can help—but can also be annoying and perceived as juvenile. Instead, create empathy through words rather than symbols. Start an email—particularly if it is a new exchange—with the same schmoozing that you would start a conversation. "Hi. Hope you are well. How's the summer going?" Perhaps you can refer back to your last interaction ("It was great to meet you last May at the conference") or last communication ("Thank you for your letter last week"). Think of the first paragraph of an email as an opportunity to introduce yourself before getting down to business. (This empathy creation is stronger if you have already met face-to-face or on Skype or have had a phone call, so consider starting with that mode.) The end of an email is another opportunity to create empathy with words: share something about yourself or sign off with more than your name.

This all connects to social intuition, as you need to stay attuned to how the communication is occurring. Your choice of communication mode should be highly influenced by your attention to the emotional tenor of the negotiation. Email negotiations—and the fact that we don't know when someone will receive the email, when that person is going to respond, or what he or she is thinking— can be fraught with miscommunication, so part of social intuition in using email is managing your own anxiety as well as the other person's.[74] What are the expectations for responding to emails? Do others in your lab seem to respond within 24 hours, or is a more leisurely rate acceptable? Different assumptions operate in different environments. Remember that you can prompt quick response by using more than one mode—sending a long email first and then sending a quick FYI text, just to let the other person know the email is waiting. Good practice also means letting the other person know you have received his or her communication—and when you're likely to respond. If you can't provide a full answer now, say so. This does not have to take much time or many words. "I've received your email," you might reply quickly by email, "but I need to talk to my chair before I can get back to you. I'll be in touch soon. Thanks much."

One final note on social intuition: when you are worried about the tone of an email or text that you are going to send, stop. Reread it as if you were an angry or suspicious recipient. Could your counterpart misinterpret your tone? And when reading an email that you have received and are starting to interpret in a bad way, try rereading the email assuming that your counterpart is happy with you. Show the email to a friend to get a different perspective. Before starting down the spiral of angry exchanges, make sure you want to engage in that way. Sometimes, stepping away from the computer for a few hours or sending your preferred (obnoxious, witty, awesome comeback) email response to yourself only will help you blow off steam and find the equilibrium you need.

Pros and Cons of Each Mode of Communication

	PROS	CONS
Face-to-face conversation (in-person and videoconference)	Allows for tracking of multiple social cues (i.e., interpret body language, tone, eye contact, and facial expressions)	Limited time to develop a response
Phone call	Allows for tracking of certain social cues through the tone, pauses, and inflections (i.e., can learn about how the other party is feeling) Synchronous communication (i.e., ability to explain in real time, ask questions, and clarify ambiguities)	No chance to interpret certain important social cues (i.e., body language, eye contact, and facial expressions)
Email	Flexibility of choosing when to read and respond Ability to reread and reflect before responding Good for task-oriented communications	Does not incorporate contextual elements (i.e., can misread social cues) Asynchronous communication (i.e., potential for slow response time and communication stack-up) Certain mirroring skills are impossible (i.e., body language, level of eye contact, and nodding) Developing trust is difficult (i.e., higher potential for deceptive practices) Difficult to demonstrate empathy
Text message	Same pros as email, except less formal	Same cons as email, except less formal Harder to keep a record of communication Easier to miss or lose thread

Choosing your mode of communication is just as important as any other challenge in your negotiation. Each mode can play to your strengths (or weaknesses); can be more persuasive (or less); and can build relationships (or tear them down). Thinking carefully about this element of negotiation will add to your effectiveness—and your ability.

CHAPTER 10
Multiparty Negotiation

Sometimes you enter into a negotiation with many people at the same time, perhaps coauthoring discussions, for which everyone is seated around a table. Other times, these negotiations are more of a sequence: first you talk to your chair, then your principle investigator, then another colleague of similar rank, and perhaps others. In one group meeting or in sequential conversations with several people, the concept and complications of multiparty negotiation are important to understand.

What Do Multiparty Negotiations Mean?

While the primary focus of this book is on negotiations involving a single counterpart, you will surely find yourself negotiating with several people, and your negotiation behavior needs to take account how these discussions differ from one-on-one situations. Perhaps many people are negotiating over one item all at the same time, for example, trying to get more lab space or working out details of coauthoring an article. Other times, you will be negotiating as part of a team, perhaps speaking to authorities about lab space on behalf of all of the people on your grant.

And yet other times, you might be facing a team of people as an individual—think about appearing before hiring committees or making grant reports. If, for example, several researchers get together to submit a program grant, they might first need to negotiate among themselves for turf and then together present the case that they are the best team. How you communicate may or may not directly change because of these group dynamics. As with the modes of communication discussed in the previous chapter, you should purposively think about how the skills of negotiation are best utilized when the dynamics are different.

Multiparty Dynamics

The first item to contemplate in multiparty negotiations is whether you have any natural allies. Building coalitions in advance of—or during—the meeting can help make you a more effective negotiator.[75] These one-on-one negotiations in advance of any multiparty negotiation could be even more important than the multiparty meeting, so thinking about your interests, the other parties' interests, and where they overlap is an investment worth making ahead of time, especially if you can plan to have another voice backing your own opinions. When you lobby in advance, you may discover that others' interests are not aligned with yours, information that is also valuable to have in advance.

Second, when you are speaking in a multiparty negotiation, you want to think about whom you are addressing. Are you speaking to persuade a dissenter? Are you speaking to persuade someone who is on the fence? Or are you "fighting the good fight," even though you know your opinion may not carry the day? When trying to persuade just one person in a face-to-face conversation, your tone and emotional level may vary over time, since you expect more give-and-take throughout the conversation. In a faculty meeting, on the other hand, you might have the chance to speak only once or twice, so what you say and how you say it should be more carefully thought out. Will your passion for a position sound committed or desperate? In these group situations, you should carefully consider your prospective audience.

Third, recognize that in a multiparty negotiation, someone present might have little (or no) interest in making a deal. Perhaps this person is annoyed because he never received such benefits. (Andrea knows this very well from personal experience. Early in her career, a female associate dean told Andrea that she really did not need a maternity leave, since the associate dean had not received one herself 30 years earlier. Luckily, the dean was less personally invested— and more accommodating.) Perhaps the uninterested party is unhappy with your mentor. Maybe she is playing interdepartmental politics, or maybe he just doesn't want to help out because he doesn't want the extra work it will bring. If you had sought out each attendee before the actual negotiation, you might have learned about these factors and been able to address them ahead of time or in the implementation plan for anything that is agreed to in the meeting. Even just identifying a "spoiler" to others in advance can be helpful in minimizing that person's role or influence.

Finally, remember that the multiparty dynamic might need to be changed. If the group is not accomplishing what you need, you might want to consider moving back to a series of one-on-one negotiations.[76] In the case of discussing coauthorship, perhaps you can start with a series of individual meetings or phone calls with potential coauthors. Then, after getting everyone on board, you can confirm your understanding with all parties together to create group buy-in.

Multiparty Negotiation Skills

Becoming good at multiparty dealings requires extra work, because you will need to consider each of the basic skills covered so far—assertiveness, empathy, flexibility, social intuition, ethical behavior, and effective communication—in light of the group situation.

For assertiveness, focusing on your priorities is particularly helpful. With limited time to speak, you will want to channel your energies to the interests that are most important to you. What are your key goals for this group interaction?

A particularly useful avenue of assertiveness in multiparty situations can be the agenda. If you have suffered through meetings that seem to be endless, accomplish little, or are dominated by one or two people, you know how agonizing such things can be. Your avenue out of this rut is to think carefully about how the meeting might be run best—and how can you help make that happen. The four P's can help organize your thoughts:[77]

Purpose. What is the purpose of this meeting?

People. For that purpose, who should be at this meeting (and who should not)?

Product. For that purpose, what is the desired outcome of this meeting? What will happen when you leave?

Process. Considering all of the above, what process do you need to accomplish the purpose and ensure the product is the result?

If you are a junior colleague, you might not be in charge of who gets invited or even when the meeting is called, but agenda-setting can be a quiet way to exert power over your time. (Once again, Andrea can testify to this: As a junior faculty member, she regularly offered to take notes and send out the advance agenda for the hiring committee. This helped keep her in the loop and allowed her to be the committee's "historian.") When it comes to multiparty negotiations, agenda-setting can be your most assertive move.

Under the skill of empathy, preparing to empathize with more than one person will take time. Depending on the size of the group, how important the issue is, and your own time constraints, you will be more effective when you can predict how others will feel about the issue at hand. This preparation is similar to what you would do before a one-on-one negotiation, but now you must multiply your effort and assess how each individual will feel about different issues. While thinking about your counterparts, be sure to flag issues where you are likely to have common as well as divergent interests.

Multiparty negotiations are often multi-issue, which can make the skill of remaining flexible about the outcome, of trying to find different ways to meet your needs, very important. Because groups inevitably need to compromise to find common ground and address many concerns, your ability to brainstorm in advance will help you feel prepared and confident as the ideas fly around the room. Consider even orchestrating group brainstorming.[78] You can help direct the whole group to better options using your flexibility skills.

Multiparty negotiations also often call on your skills of process flexibility—recognizing that you may need to use different approaches with different people—to be persuasive. Similarly, as the meeting proceeds or the series of meetings unfold, to be most effective, you may need to vary negotiation approaches.

Finally, the need for social intuition is very high in multiparty negotiations. Obviously, if the meeting subject is not that important to you, you may choose to play more of a bystander role in the negotiation. On the other hand, when the outcome matters to you, your social intuition skills will help you determine when to speak up. Tracking the body language and visual cues of all of the participants in the meeting can be challenging—but worth the effort. Have you ever been in a meeting in which someone speaks—and everyone else in the room visibly cringes? Your social intuition can save you from being that person. Think carefully about what prompts this kind of cringing: Is the point the person made already obvious? Have others already said exactly the same thing? Is the argument too self-interested or part of an agenda? To avoid prompting this reaction, craft your remarks carefully in group meetings with an eye toward assertiveness. What is your main point? What are two or three supporting arguments? Why does this make sense for the group? Speaking efficiently and in a linear fashion will help your arguments stand out from the many other comments that are usually shared during multiparty negotiations. Remember that as the number of participants increases, the likelihood of a real negotiation decreases. In faculty meetings, for example, the real negotiations are often on the committee level, with the larger group expected only to rubber-stamp the committee's recommendations.

Being part of multiparty negotiations requires you to use all the negotiation skills you normally bring to bear plus more attention to the group dynamics. In advance of the negotiation, think carefully about researching your counterparts, schmoozing, and meeting with them and also about some subtle lobbying. During the negotiation, watch carefully how the interaction goes, tracking social intuition so you can be flexible in approach and outcome. Ensuring compliance in these multiparty negotiations can be challenging, so make sure the tasks and deadlines for each participant are clear so that your goals are accomplished. And be sure to focus on follow-up, so that something actually gets done.

INSPIRATION
development
support
networking

CHAPTER 11
Mentors

You might wonder why we have included a chapter in mentoring in a book about negotiation in academia and scientific arenas.

As earlier chapters noted, you have used all your negotiating styles and skills in a variety of settings throughout your personal and professional life. You learned these negotiation skills by observing others, which includes watching your mentor negotiate with others, including you.

Because mentors play such important, necessary, and often complicated roles in our personal and professional lives, the topic of mentors and mentoring merits inclusion in any discussion about how to accomplish your goals in your profession. You can learn about negotiation from your mentor in at least two ways—by watching him or her negotiate with others and from your own experience of sitting in the other chair at the negotiation table, negotiating with your mentor. In other words, you've seen her ski down trails, and she has also been the one to design ski trails for you.

Given the complexity of academic life, separating career advancement and mentoring is virtually impossible. Mentoring—and having a mentor—have always been important in any professional sphere, but only in recent decades have these topics received considerable attention and study from observers and scholars, most of whom now consider mentoring an essential part of career development. The academic literature is now filled with articles devoted to mentoring. (Note that in this context, we are not examining the basic importance of mentoring, supervising, and training but rather are focusing only on mentoring as one of the crucial arenas where negotiation occurs.)

Mentoring has become such an accepted concept and process that the phrase has worked its way into our everyday vocabulary and taken on many informal meanings. For this book's purposes, mentoring refers to the set of relationships that are often initiated and developed in academic and personal life and are an integral part of the career trajectory.

If you accept the notion of mentoring over your entire career cycle, you will realize that by the time you think you need a mentor, you have probably already had several. You did not necessarily label them mentors, nor did you even think about the relationship in a traditional mentor/mentee sense, but as in so many areas of life, this kind of early imprinting is worth some analysis. (In animal behavior, "imprinting" specifically refers to the rapid learning that occurs during a brief receptive period, typically soon after birth or hatching, and establishes a long-lasting behavioral response to a specific individual or object. A baby chick that sees its mother shortly after hatching, for example, tends to follow that hen and mimic its behavior.) In many ways, your first mentor represents your first good or bad work negotiation experience, and that relationship may play an outsized role in setting up your future expectations.

Some observers have written that having a good mentor early in your career may mean the difference between success and failure in any field, and some recommend spending enough "investigative" time to ensure that you find a "mentor for life." But as an article published in *Nature* several years ago indicated, many aspects of mentoring can influence your career,[79] and as two who have worked in academia for many decades, being mentored and mentoring, we firmly do not believe that one mentor is all you need for your entire academic life.

Instead, we believe that the mentoring role and what those being mentored need change over time, so you should periodically assess all aspects of your mentor/mentee relationships. Recognize also that mentoring is different from coaching or from having someone act as your sponsor. A mentor need not be your supervisor, and you may be better off if he or she is not.

In assessing mentor/mentee relationships and their quality, you will benefit from reviewing some key characteristics you want in a mentor (which incidentally are not so different from the basic skills such as empathy and flexibility). You might want to organize them into a few sections: the personal characteristics of a mentor; the mentor's availability; your skill development; and networking. A review of the table below[80] provides the key ingredients of the mentor-mentee relationship and its development. For an especially successful relationship, look for components from all four dimensions.

What is a Good Mentor?

PERSONAL CHARACTERISTICS OF AN IDEAL MENTOR

- Enthusiasm/passion
- Sensitivity
- Appreciation of individual differences
- Respect
- Unselfishness
- Support for people and things other than his or her own work

AVAILABILITY/HELPFULNESS/SUPPORTIVENESS

- Has an "open door" policy
- Is consistent in offering inspiration and optimism
- Is able to balance directing and allowing self-direction
- Is skilled in the art of questioning and listening
- Is widely read and widely receptive
- Offers an initiation project (your first "collaborative" activity)

- Is helpful in discussing life after science
- Is able to help with celebration

YOUR SKILL DEVELOPMENT BASED ON MENTOR/MENTEE INTERACTION AND EXPERIENCES

- Criticism
- Writing
- Oral presentation

NETWORKING

- Use of his or her contacts and relationships with students and young staff
- Help with and introductions to presentations and meetings
- Advice on career decisions

This set of attributes and activities, while not complete, does tend to idealize the notion of a mentor. While many of these attributes are important, depending on where you are in the life cycle of your career, you will have more (or less) need for particular skills and interactions. Furthermore, no one human being is likely to have all these attributes.

In the beginning of your career, for example, you will probably look for someone who conveys a high level of passion and enthusiasm and has open-door availability. If you have a hard time getting a regular appointment time and prompt feedback, then you may have difficulty both setting and achieving goals, even an initial set of goals. If you cannot meet or talk with your mentor with some level of regularity, perhaps the person does not have the time—or the emotional space—to mentor someone. Of course, mentor/mentee relationships are two-way streets when it comes to communication and responsibility, but especially with your early experiences, a certain level of chemistry between you and your mentor should be apparent to both.

In thinking about your mentor and negotiation, remember your basic skills and the five different areas of potential negotiation styles highlighted in earlier chapters. You may want to use your mentoring relationship as relatively safe space for practicing negotiating activities so that you will be better prepared for real-life negotiations. If your mentor has reasonable negotiation skills, take advantage of your time together and observe how he or she negotiates with you and with others. (If he or she is not a great role model in this area, check the later chapter that deals with "divorcing" your mentor, which is a challenging negotiation indeed.)

Each major move you make in your career is a good time to reassess your relationship with your mentor. For your next step, do you need a new mentor? Or an additional one, someone who has not been part of your support team so far? As you develop, you will notice a constant mentor-mentee tension between your need for direction and need for independence. You will also want something far less concrete from an effective mentor: the ability to challenge and stimulate your thinking, which in the long run will constitute your creativity.

Just as with other negotiation skills, consider setting goals for your relationship with your mentor or mentors. Your success will be linked to passion, persistence, and enthusiasm—traits that you and your mentor should share. You should also plan for open communication and recognize that the mentee-mentor relationship will likely use all five aspects of negotiating style over time. Perhaps most important, especially for helping you grow and learn to mentor others, an effective mentor will help you build your own professional networks.

Returning to the analogy of skiing and ski trails, the goal of this relationship is to help you navigate all kinds of trails. Before you slide into your brand-new boots, step onto shiny skis, and grab some poles for the first time, you will probably want to consider taking some lessons. Maybe you will sign up for group lessons, or maybe you know you will do better with individual instruction. What kind of teacher can you best learn from? Who can show you how it's done? How to get up after a painful fall? Taking extra time now in making this choice will ensure that your mentor is a good instructor and role model.

CHAPTER 12 | PART TWO: REAL-LIFE SCENARIOS
PhD Thesis (or the Equivalent Advanced Degree)

Authors' note: The following chapter starts a new section of this book. Understanding and discussing theory are important and certainly the least painful and most time-efficient ways to start learning a new skills or skills. But you live in the real world, encountering situations in which you have goals, hopes, and dreams, and you will face challenges trying to realize them. Because putting negotiation skills into practice and advancing your career are your goals, in this portion of the book, Chapters 12 through 21, we switch to sketching out career situations that are as close to real life as we can make them. These examples spring from our own experiences (some David's, some Andrea's, some a blend) and from those of people we have worked with. We hope that in them you will recognize something of yourself and turning points in your career.

The formula for all scenarios is the same: we set out the situation; look at how someone might prepare for the particular context, size up his or her counterpart, and choose a negotiation style or styles; and then examine possible outcomes and lessons.

Scenario

By all accounts—his own, his professors', and even many of his colleagues'—Andrew has a promising future.

Andrew received his undergraduate degree in psychology from a highly regarded school in the East six years ago, and he is now working on his doctorate at a top-ranked university in the Midwest. He has generally gotten along well with Jonathan, his PhD advisor, whose area of expertise is close (but not identical) to Andrew's own specialty. In the first years of their relationship things went well, and Jonathan was great at helping Andrew adjust to life in a new department, new university, and even a new climate. But sometime around his third year of graduate school, Andrew noticed that Jonathan kept assigning him tasks that were not at all related to Andrew's dissertation, and carrying out these assignments is now keeping Andrew from making significant progress toward his graduate degree. Now, in his sixth year of grad school, Andrew is still working on his PhD. Like many others, Andrew's university has a limitation on how long he can take to complete his dissertation and still graduate with a doctorate. There are other complications: the members of his dissertation committee have started openly disagreeing, infighting that even extends to what each one thinks of Andrew's progress. Some members of the committee, for example, have pushed him to change his thesis topic on three separate occasions. Meanwhile, Andrew's graduate-school debts are piling up, no new fellowship or extension of his current fellowship is available, and he knows he cannot get an academic job until he completes his dissertation. In short, something needs to change. Soon.

Preparing for the Context

Before deciding what to do next, Andrew should look at how he got into this situation in the first place. If he is being honest with himself, Andrew has to acknowledge that he has been accommodating his advisor and his committee for years. In addition, Andrew has avoided directly confronting them, hoping they will realize that time is running out for him to complete his dissertation.

Now he is under considerable pressure to graduate, and he knows that to get the kind of teaching position he wants, he will ultimately need recommendations from his advisor and members of the dissertation committee. With all this in mind, Andrew needs to prepare to act and negotiate with a strategy that is different from his usual, take-it-easy way. He will need to improve his level of empathy and flexibility. But before doing so, he needs to gather some information.

Specifically, he needs the answers to four questions. What is his advisor's track record with other students? What are the university's rules for dissertation completion and graduation? What are the rules for changing dissertation advisors? With whom (among the faculty or in the university administration) can Andrew discuss such issues openly?

ANDREW'S GOALS

Issue	Completing Phd Thesis (or the Equivalent Advanced Degree)
Other Parties	Jonathan, Andrew's Advisor; Andrew's Other Thesis Committee Members
Goals	Action
Specific	Andrew needs to: Outline remaining tasks to complete his dissertation and create a completion timeline Prepare and schedule a meeting with his advisor within the next two weeks with the objective of creating a mutually agreeable plan for moving forward Create a game plan for addressing conflict in similar situations (i.e., those where pressure builds quickly)
Aspirational	Jonathan understands where Andrew is coming from and stops giving him such a heavy workload
Reasonable	Andrew needs to be aware and understand that there is a delicate balance between his personal needs and what his advisor (or others in the department) might need

Assessing the Counterpart

Before sitting down with anyone, Andrew will benefit from reviewing how his advisor and other members of his dissertation committee usually operate. Once again, specific questions help: How have these people typically dealt with him? Do they sheepishly ask for help, or are they demanding? Do they behave this way with all their graduate students, or just with Andrew? Has Andrew become their workhorse or doormat? Have other students come and gone within a relatively short period? Has Andrew's own advisor purposefully taken advantage of him? In summary, what "negotiation styles" do his advisors generally employ with Andrew and his peers?

Possible Approaches

Looking critically at this chronic and ongoing reality, Andrew knows he has to do something before the situation implodes and he finds himself having wasted many years.

Finally, after much thought, Andrew concludes that he has at least four immediate options. He could change his advisor. The second option, Andrew decides, is to seek outside consultation with senior faculty, including members of his dissertation committee. If he's inclined to think about the skiing analogy, Andrew might well see the options before him as all difficult, black-diamond trails, loaded with danger and unexpected bumps that could cause serious injury. But he should also remember that preparation makes a huge difference in performance—and that on even the steepest mountain a skier will find an occasional gentle and easy stretch. He has been on green trails too long, and that is what has gotten him to this place. He could decide to not complete any task that is not directly related to his dissertation. He could set up a meeting with Jonathan, his advisor, to develop a firm timeline and prioritize all the tasks and responsibilities that must be completed before he can finish his dissertation.

Andrew realizes that he can pursue more than one of these options—and that he may want to carry them out in a sequential manner. Choosing which approach to use when, however, will require some self-examination and self-awareness.

Andrew has felt uncomfortable being assertive his entire life, preferring to avoid head-on confrontations and hoping crises will just blow over eventually, but he knows that this situation requires some level of assertiveness. And he knows that figuring out what to do in what order requires an increased degree of flexibility. Such a delicate—yet pressing—problem requires high levels of understanding of himself and others. Yes, Andrew could find a new advisor, but cutting the umbilical cord that ties him to Jonathan is no easy matter. Whichever route he takes, Andrew's usual comfort zone, avoidance, will not work in this situation (and, he is forced to admit, contributed to the mess he's in now). Perhaps a better choice would be to accommodate Jonathan (assuming that keeping his advisor happy is something Andrew sees as valuable), in which case Andrew probably will need to invest a tremendous amount of time and energy in charting a new plan in collaboration with Jonathan. Or he could spend what will probably be an equally tremendous amount of time building a new relationship with a new advisor. Either way, Andrew will need empathy and social intuition.

Outcomes

 In finalizing his approach and looking at the possible outcome, Andrew needs to review the advantages and disadvantages of each option. If he decided to change advisors, to make the case for this move, Andrew would need to change, becoming assertive and adopting a competing style, since Jonathan is not likely to take this rejection passively and Andrew might well have to do some serious convincing to get another professor to sign on as his advisor at this late date. While switching advisors could allow Andrew to finish his dissertation and graduate, doing so would probably make enemies, burn bridges, and taint Andrew's (so far good) reputation. If Andrew had the support of other faculty besides Jonathan, a switch might also endanger that goodwill. Hence, the second option of talking with other faculty or the dissertation committee must also be pursued carefully, with serious attention paid to the varying and conflicting interests of that group and the politics of the department. (Note the lessons from the multiparty chapter—the number of parties alone could make this a black-diamond trail, since their conflicting and hidden agendas could be unseen moguls.) And what about the worst outcome? What if Jonathan cannot sign up a new advisor and his dissertation gets completely derailed?

The third option, not completing tasks assigned by Jonathan that do not relate to Andrew's dissertation, might appeal for several reasons, including the fact that avoiding is Andrew's default style. One advantage of this strategy could be that Andrew would have more time to finish his dissertation and/or that this quiet refusal would prompt Jonathan to raise the issue of time allocation and discuss how Andrew spends his hours. If Jonathan is also an avoider (or is too busy to deal with Andrew), this approach could work out well. Avoiding, in short, might save the day.

But this option could also blow up in Andrew's face. Jonathan, angered by unfinished tasks, could confront Andrew and then give him more work that impedes Andrew's dissertation progress. If Jonathan is assertive, competitive, and accustomed to having Andrew doing exactly as he is told, simply not doing what Jonathan asks could spell disaster.

In following the last strategy, setting up a meeting with Jonathan to develop a timeline and prioritize responsibilities, Andrew would be accommodating. Hoping that Jonathan can be collaborative, Andrew would seek to be quite problem-focused and work toward a good solution for all. But in taking this approach, Andrew clearly would need to be creative and flexible.

The collaborative option could have several advantages. It would allow Andrew to be transparent about exactly what he needs to get done—and why and when. Perhaps Jonathan is genuinely unaware of Andrew's concerns, and if he knew more, could or would empathize with Andrew's situation. If they sat down and worked out a plan of action they both could sign onto, that might well enhance Andrew's chances of success, since people generally tend to have a greater stake in agreements they were involved in crafting.

On the other hand, there are several possible disadvantages: perhaps Jonathan does care about his time pressure and would accuse Andrew of whining or procrastinating. Another possibility is that Andrew makes a plan but cannot or does not carry it out.

Lessons

 This scenario illustrates several points worth remembering. First, regarding advisors, Andrew would have done well to do some research as soon as he arrived at his new university, talking with new colleagues and professors before choosing his own advisor. Second, timing is important. If Andrew is going to change advisors, he should do so sooner rather than later. Finally, to protect his reputation, he needs to examine things carefully, weighing the value of completing his work and his reputation as a trustworthy colleague. His perspective should be broad, since Andrew should also be thinking about how his conflict patterns play out over time.

Accommodating often looks appealing because it appears to put an end to a conflict. But sometimes it can lead to the complete ignoring of your needs, which can make things even worse. Because Andrew took so long to pursue his own crucial interests, he has made achieving those interests far more difficult. If this is a pattern, behavior he repeats with other people in other situations, Andrew should take stock and consider whether it's time for him to change his ways. Recognizing a conflict when it begins and raising his concerns promptly, Andrew might find, make his life—and his downhill trails—a lot easier.

CHAPTER 13
Fellowship/Post-Doctoral Training

Scenario

Congratulations are in order.

Lucy has just received her PhD from a large university, the same school where she got her undergraduate degree. Now she's ready to begin her search for the best, most appropriate post-doctoral training. One initial question is whether she should stay in the same location for this next career step, an idea she sees as having both advantages and drawbacks. In addition to being uncertain about where she should be, Lucy is unsure about whether she should apply for a slot in a formal post-doc training program or find an individual post-doc position in a specific laboratory with a specific mentor. She has had mixed experiences with her supervisors to date, so the mentor/boss/supervisor question is a particularly perplexing one.

Preparing for the Context

A post-doctoral experience with a possible fellowship, Lucy knows, represents something very important. This next step may help her eventually get a faculty position, which is her ultimate goal. She also understands that a fellowship offers other vital opportunities to focus and develop specific expertise in one area, which will be essential in winning a faculty position anywhere.

She knows, too, that this next phase will require a high level of sustained assertiveness, a trait that will also help her obtain grants. So her strategy must involve setting very specific goals, ones that she can prioritize in creating an optimistic and justifiable plan for a career trajectory.

Particularly because she does not yet know whom she will be dealing with, Lucy's approach will have to be creative and flexible. Whatever negotiating style she will eventually choose will depend on the decision-makers wherever she applies for a position—all of which underscores the importance of carefully researching each location she intends to consider.

Once Lucy begins to do her homework on each place she might apply, she will want to assess each department's or institution's overall environment. What is the track record of each? What happens to the post-docs who work there? Do any of them stay and join the faculty? How are the fellows "used," and what is the workplace "climate?" If she has enough time and energy to visit or contact people who know the departments or labs, she can also assess levels of collaboration and how empathetic potential mentors seem at each place.

In assessing each location and environment, Lucy needs to think about how each one might (or might not) dovetail with her personal life. She thinks she will soon have to make a decision about a relationship. She has been dating someone for five years, living with him for more than a year, and in recent conversations the two have talked candidly about their next step. Should they marry? Stay together but not marry? Part for some time and see what happens? And, of course, she is wondering about other factors connected to geography. How far away from her parents and siblings does she want to be? If she is used to city life, how will she take to a rural setting? How much snow is she willing to shovel?

LUCY'S GOALS

Issue	Fellowship / Post-Doctroral Training
Other Parties	Lucy's Peers; her Advisors; and her Partner

GOALS	ACTION
	Lucy should:
	Narrow her list down to three institutions
	Talk to at least three to five peers and advisors for advice
Specific	Set her priorities in terms of salary, start-up costs for lab, and advising
	Make a final decision within the hiring season
Aspirational	Plan to ask at the high-end for her start-up package cost and salary
Reasonable	Recognize tradeoffs in priorities–e.g., know one position might be perfect in one area, but not another

Assessing the Counterpart

As Lucy carries out her investigations of possible locations for next year, she will need to prepare for interviews at specific institutions. This requires extensive reading of the primary papers of possible supervisors. How are these individuals recognized in their own field? Have many of these potential supervisors moved around over a period of several years? Looking at their movements should give Lucy a sense of how stable each environment is. She should try to listen to their presentations, through webinars if not in person. Lucy needs to travel, too: she needs to meet people, look them in the eye, and get a sense of them—use her social intuition—before she makes any kind of commitment. On her visits, she will want to speak to peers in similar situations and assess the environment, including how people collaborate with supervisors and with one another. Based on the current group of fellows, how competitive does each specific program appear?

So how can Lucy figure out the best alternatives? She should develop a list of the best places in her overall area of training and identify the top individuals in each university or training facility, a task that will require considerable research. Aside from the academic issues and the quality of the faculty and the institution, Lucy will want to consider what kind of skills she herself will need—or need to develop—in moving to a new location. Uprooting herself and starting fresh will require considerable negotiation and the need to be assertive, creative, and flexible. Lucy may also need to assess the "ideal" aspects of her potential colleagues, not just whether they will be good bosses or mentors but whether they will provide the flexible and collaborative approach that she wants.

Possible Approaches

 Having spent considerable time studying other settings, Lucy realizes that one option is to accept a post-doc position at her current institution. This would certainly be easier and quicker to negotiate, a relatively easy beginner slope. Because she has been at the school for many years, however, she might need to compromise. Also, because everyone knows her, she might find assuming a new role at the same place much more difficult than she would if she were a newcomer, and if she has not been particularly confident or forceful before, she might find becoming more assertive equally challenging.

In assessing the merits of staying put, Lucy will want to use her list of needs to develop a reasonable offer for herself and probably work it out with individuals she knows reasonably well. On the other hand, in working out a position elsewhere, to get what she wants, she will need to place a premium on assertiveness and adopt a competitive style. With much research, careful planning, and perhaps a little luck, she will have several offers to compare and use to negotiate a boost in the offer from her top choice.

Outcomes

After 10 years, Lucy is really inclined to leave her current environment. While it is familiar, it has also become boring, and she is looking for a new challenge. Lucy also just learned that her favorite advisor is retiring within the next six months, and many of the other faculty members she might want to align herself with are not interested in mentoring her because they already have other mentees—or so it looks to Lucy now. Nevertheless, Lucy realizes that staying put should remain an option and she should gather information about the department's history of hiring faculty from outside, rather than promoting its own students, just as she has with other departments at other schools. Her boyfriend is also finishing his degree and will be looking for a job, but he has said he is willing to move with Lucy to another city. So she has spent the last month compiling considerable information about 10 institutions throughout the United States. Lucy has also identified key faculty at each place, has attended several meetings to introduce herself, and has listened to talks by eight faculty members. In addition, she has located webinars from six other faculty members. At the same time, she has tried to take into account their geographic setting, eliminating two places because their climate is similar to what she has experienced over the last decade. In assessing advantages and disadvantages of each of the 10 places and reducing the list to six, Lucy has sought to balance academic quality, faculty, and the workplace ethos.

The next step is for Lucy to visit the six places and use the checklist she developed for possible advantages and disadvantages—after which she narrows down her list to four schools. Next comes a second visit to her top-three choices, this time with her boyfriend.

Through all this, Lucy has watched herself rise to the occasion—buckling down to do the difficult background research and becoming more assertive than ever before. She has realized that she is competing for positions with others who are quite assertive, and she knows that to sell herself and lock in an offer, she needs to strongly outline her research, her strengths, and her record. In just a short time, studying and weighing all her options, Lucy is becoming much more comfortable in her new garb as a competitive person.

Lessons

 One hallmark of Lucy's experience is the amount of time and energy that figuring things out can take. Visiting each location took both time and money, but the investment was a good one because it paid big dividends in terms of information. Seeing a lab up close and talking to a post-doc over coffee helped Lucy sense firsthand what working there would be like.

The decision-making process took longer and was harder and the need to balance work and personal life took on greater meaning than Lucy had imagined they would, but the value of all her hard work is clear: Lucy feels much more comfortable at the end of the process than she did at the beginning. She is pleased that she finally took some risks in considering a move after 10 years, paying great attention to setting and prioritizing her own goals and needs. In the end, research and consideration that took longer than she ever expected could save her years of having to work in a place where she isn't happy.

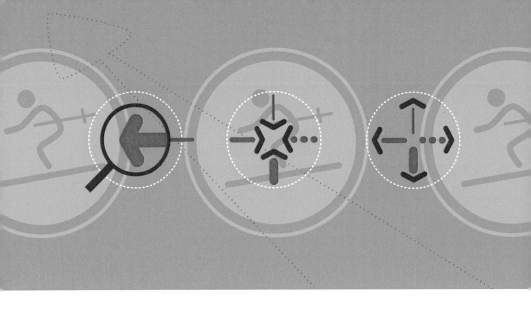

CHAPTER 14
Authorship

Scenario

Zoe is always up for a challenge, but she's surprised—and unsure—about this one.

A fellow at a medium-size university in the South, Zoe has spent her first and second academic years settling in, learning how her colleagues operate, doing her own work, and getting to know her mentor, Madeleine. Regular monthly meetings have helped both of them slide into a relationship that is both professional and cordial. Zoe greatly admires Madeleine, who has done impressive work in their field, and she is pleased to think that the two women have learned to talk with some ease in a relatively short time. But the ending of their most recent meeting was a shock.

In their monthly meeting, Madeleine had told Zoe that she needed to put higher priority on completing and submitting two manuscripts summarizing new and exciting findings from her dissertation research and a subsequent follow-up study. Zoe agreed with her mentor that getting two more first-author papers published within the next year is very important, since Zoe is working on a proposal for a research career development award, a grant specifically aimed at helping young scientists pursue their work. Two published papers, especially in such a short time, would show Zoe's productivity and expertise in an area that is an essential foundation for where she wants to go.

Then, speaking casually but clearly, Madeleine told Zoe that about a month ago, another prominent researcher in their field at another university, Professor Holland, had asked Madeleine to write a chapter on recent scientific advances for an updated edition of Holland's very popular textbook. Because she thinks so highly of Holland and knows she can make a meaningful contribution to what is likely to be an important, widely circulated work, Madeleine said, she quickly agreed to Holland's request. But when she returned to her office, Madeleine said, she promptly got caught up in an especially busy fall, and she hasn't written a word for the book. Now her chapter is overdue. Would Zoe like to work on this project with Madeleine over the next few weeks? Zoe was completely taken aback and ducked the question. But Madeleine needs an answer.

Madeleine will be Zoe's primary mentor on the proposed grant award proposal, and Zoe wants to make sure to stay in her good graces so she will give Zoe a strong recommendation and endorsement. One last factor to consider is that Zoe also greatly admires Professor Holland, the editor of the book, and considers her a leader in Zoe's field. In fact, many of Professor Holland's books were required reading in Zoe's own training.

Preparing for the Context

 As Zoe begins to assess her mentor's proposal, she realizes that despite the rapport she thought she had with Madeleine, Zoe does not really completely understand her mentor, how Madeleine thinks, and the surprising way Madeleine popped this proposal. Zoe has always been candid and open with Madeleine, so she thinks a discussion of multiple solutions is a good idea.

Zoe also now sees that when Madeleine brought up the coauthor idea, Zoe was too surprised to think of an appropriate response—and when she thinks about this some more, she realizes that this is not the first time Madeleine has made a request out of the blue. Zoe knows she ducked the coauthor question, pleading for more time to think about it, but perhaps this will work out: avoiding isn't her usual style, but this way she can think carefully, formulate a good response, and return to the negotiation table much better prepared.

This offer does warrant some attention, since Holland is the major figure in this specific area. The clock is ticking; Zoe has only one more year to build her reputation and improve the chances that this fellowship will be a springboard to a research faculty position. Zoe needs to evaluate her priorities carefully and become more reflective about this situation.

ZOE'S GOALS

Issue	Authorship
Other Parties	Madeleine, Zoe's Mentor

GOALS	ACTION
	Zoe needs to:
	Continue working on the two first-author papers that she hopes to get published within the next year
	Continue to work on the research career development award proposal that she hopes to get funded
Specific	Calculate how much time it will take to figure out the contribution to the Holland book chapter and how manageable that time demand will be
	Stay in Madeleine's good graces (if she wants Madeleine to recommend her and endorse her award proposal)
	Get a clearer understanding of Madeleine—how she thinks and why she brought up the chapter as she did. Any workable plan to understand Madeleine better needs specific steps and a way to measure Zoe's progress
Aspirational	Zoe should ask for coauthorship on the chapter
Reasonable	Zoe needs to plan to work with her mentor to set out a time frame (or game plan) for balancing the four projects: getting two articles published under Zoe's own name, writing the chapter for Holland's book, and working on her career development grant proposal

Assessing the Counterpart

To make an informed decision, Zoe will need to perform "due diligence" on the first edition of the book edited by Professor Holland. How well did that first edition do when it was first published? Is the book still prominent in Zoe's own field? If Zoe chooses to pursue the invitation, what is the likelihood that she will be able to network with other book contributors and even Holland herself?

Zoe should give herself a second assignment: carefully review Madeleine's curriculum vitae to see whether other mentees have received coauthorships for chapters—and whether granting authorships or coauthorships is a regular practice for Madeleine. Zoe also might want to check out Madeleine's work habits on similar assignments. Does she routinely push deadlines? If she is working with a coauthor, does she require a rough draft or a completely polished piece? Extensive homework will pay off: Zoe is making decisions that will affect her own career, so she will want to know in advance if someone works in a way that will make it hard for Zoe to achieve her own goals in a timely fashion without excessive aggravation.

Possible Approaches

First and foremost, Zoe realizes that maintaining a good working relationship with her mentor Madeleine is vital. Flexibility will help ensure an outcome that makes both parties happy; as she thinks about how best to respond to Madeleine's surprising request and its possible impact on Zoe's work, Zoe will want to consider several options. One is to agree to work on the book chapter, with or without authorship, in addition to completing the two manuscripts directly related to Zoe's own work and hope Madeleine grants coauthorship to her anyway. A second choice would be to explicitly ask for coauthorship on the book chapter. Zoe could also decline to do the chapter for Holland's book.

In analyzing the range of possible responses, Zoe will see that the first option, agreeing to do the Holland chapter and continue working on her own articles, represents a straightforward accommodating style aimed at keeping Zoe's and Madeleine's relationship agreeable and supportive and to some extent, at sacrificing Zoe's own interests. This is a bunny slope negotiation—but one that could turn Zoe's workload or stress level into a black-diamond trail. The second response, in which Zoe is asking to do the book chapter as a coauthor, would require a more competitive style, one in which Zoe is seeking to be assertive and make a strong case for her own current and future position. The third response, saying no to the chapter, is essentially avoiding—although Madeleine may well see it as a competitive, selfish, or even silly choice, especially if Zoe does not explain to Madeleine that her refusal is prompted by the demands of Zoe's own work. With this in mind, Zoe may also consider having a more open conversation with Madeleine about such concerns, which would be a good example of collaboration and seeking to work out a collaborative arrangement. If Madeleine is interested in that conversation, this option may make sense. These kind of conversations, which are not direct "asks" but exploratory discussions, can be viewed as more intermediate trails. If, however, Madeleine has indicated that she wants an immediate answer, an extended conversation may not work. Collaboration takes time, and in the face of an impending deadline, it may not always be a useful strategy.

Outcomes

 As Zoe reviews the possible outcomes and decides on the best negotiating style, she could decide that compromising and looking for the middle ground may be the quickest way to get to a solution. If she agrees to work on the Holland textbook chapter, with or without authorship, in addition to continuing her own writing, Zoe can reiterate that she expects to be first author on the two other manuscripts coming from her work in the laboratory and that she expects Madeleine to help make that happen. One huge advantage of this approach is that she would please her mentor and get assistance in completing those two essential manuscripts. On the other hand, Zoe would be spending plenty of time gathering information and helping to write a chapter for which she may get no credit—and none of the professional recognition that comes with authorship.

A second tactic, one that moves the discussion more to a collaborative position, is for Zoe to insist that her work on the chapter with Madeleine merits an authorship—but one that does not detract from Madeleine's position as senior author. Zoe knows that if she turned all her attention to whatever chapter Madeleine has in mind, she and Madeleine could finish the chapter fairly quickly, and coauthorship would bring Zoe much-needed visibility. The disadvantage: because Madeleine did not mention coauthorship in her initial proposal to Zoe, such a clear demand could put Madeleine in a tough position. Madeleine definitely needs Zoe to help finish this chapter anytime soon, but she may be annoyed and might not help Zoe with Zoe's own two manuscripts. To some extent, using this tactic will depend on how well Zoe can read Madeleine. How highly tuned are Zoe's empathy and social intuition?

The third tactic, one that involves a competing style and does not provide a useful approach to resolving future similar dilemmas, is to say no to the Holland chapter. Zoe could say that she is committed to finishing up her two manuscripts as soon as possible and cannot afford any distraction. This makes sense, however, only if completing the two manuscripts is more important than Zoe's relationship with Madeleine.

Lessons

 With respect to all these discussions, Zoe will be wise to record the results of her various conversations, often following them up with email. For example, if Madeleine agrees to give Zoe a coauthorship on the chapter, Zoe might want to follow up with an email confirming this invitation. When the stakes are high, verbal agreements probably are not sufficient. In this situation, as in so many, Zoe will be much better off if she examines and ranks her interests; exercises her social intuition, assertiveness, and research skills to really understand her relationship with her mentor; and responds after taking time for careful consideration.

CHAPTER 15
How to Divorce Your Mentor and Survive

Scenario

At first, it felt like a match made in heaven.

When Noah arrived at Danielle's molecular laboratory as a young post-doctoral student just starting his fellowship, he was very excited—and especially pleased when Danielle agreed to be his mentor. He was willing to do just about anything to establish himself as a vital member of her research team, so when various opportunities came up for reviewing data or preparing papers, presentations, and chapters, Noah contributed a considerable amount of intense research work.

In turn, Danielle provided resources for Noah, counseled him about his career, and opened doors for him to meet other scientists. Coauthorship on many reports from the laboratory—and even a few first authorships—enabled Noah to rapidly develop a reasonable publication list for a young investigator. Within two years,

Noah got his first research grant, a federal career development award that allowed him to reduce his teaching load, become a junior faculty member, and continue to use Danielle's laboratory resources.

Over the next two years, however, Noah began to notice that his relationship with Danielle was changing. Securing a regular appointment time and getting feedback, formally and informally, about his own lab studies or any presentation or manuscript were difficult.

He had always understood that this relationship was a two-way street in terms of communication, but now Noah senses a new feeling of almost overt competition and a palpable tension whenever he discusses ideas, projects, and papers with Danielle. In a way, the underlying question seems to be who really "owns" the data and has the final say on authorship order—let alone whether Noah should even be a coauthor.

While Noah has been getting coauthorships, any request for senior authorship, which he feels he certainly has deserved on certain manuscripts, has been met with almost frank hostility. Now that he is preparing two grant proposals for which he has developed an independent set of research objectives, Noah is wondering whether it is time to negotiate a new mentorship relationship within the department. He still likes Danielle personally, but "doing business" with her in any kind of collaborative fashion (at least, he thought their arrangement was collaborative) is proving very difficult. In other words, each conversation feels like skiing down an expert slope in stormy conditions.

Preparing for the Context

On further reflection, Noah realizes that his persistent difficulties with Danielle, which started about nine months before, are beginning to wear on him. He is not as much fun at home; Noah's wife regularly says that he does not spend enough quality time with her, and she complains that he is always worrying about what's going on in the laboratory, particularly his relationship with Danielle. In short, Noah is taking too much workplace stuff home with him.

While Noah's career is going well and he is publishing reports in excellent peer-reviewed and high-impact journals, he is not getting enough first authorships for what he sees as the next stage of his career. Furthermore, what he is publishing is not as creative as it probably should be. (This is not just Noah's view; he remembers overhearing a comment to this effect by one of the senior researchers in the department who does not work directly with him.) This lack of creativity may ultimately affect Noah's ability to obtain independent project funding and could create barriers as he tries to establish himself and his work as independent of Danielle and her lab.

Shortly after arriving, Noah made a timeline for himself, and he thought by this time he would have a strong case to get independent laboratory space from Asher, who is chair of the department. But Noah has a way to go before being able to do such a thing. He has other worries as well: he is not going to enough national scientific meetings to present his own data, and he has not been successful in applying for memberships in several select scientific societies—a surprising development that one researcher told Noah, off the record, could be related to his close relationship with Danielle.

If he is being candid with himself, Noah sees that in the long run, his styles of avoiding and accommodating are not helping his career. He once prided himself on being way ahead of the pack. Now, he realizes, he has fallen behind.

NOAH'S GOALS

Issue	How to Divorce Your Mentor and Survive
Other Parties	Danielle, Noah's Mentor; Asher, the Chair of his Department

GOALS	ACTION
Specific	Noah needs to: Recalibrate his relationship with Danielle and determine why it has become so difficult Set up a meeting with Danielle ASAP, ideally within a week or two, to address this. He needs to be fully prepared for this meeting Talk to associates about how they have handled similar situations and ask for their advice on his situation Outline parameters on the use of data in the lab study Establish a way to communicate better with his mentor in the future Find and list three to five other people who would be good mentors and even reach out to one at the same time he talks to Danielle
Aspirational	Noah should: Aim for a resolution that will allow him to receive senior authorship while also repairing and restoring his relationship with Danielle Find a new mentor who will allow him to pursue interests in other fields, unrelated to the fields Danielle is currently involved in
Reasonable	Danielle might feel that Noah has overstepped his bounds. Noah might need to reconcile this fact and meet Danielle's concerns on certain manuscripts

Assessing the Counterparts

 The first thing Noah needs to do is find out systematically what is going on with other people in similar situations in his own department. He needs to assess their own timetables and essentially do an analysis of other colleagues with respect to their goals and where they are currently on their own trajectory, as well as honestly perform one for himself. In a sense, he must take ownership of this important career task. He needs to compare the roles and expectations of others with his own. He may conclude that he needs to be more assertive.

Noah also may want to discuss his situation with his old advisors from graduate school. Do they have suggestions with respect to job opportunities or mentors in other university settings?

Noah may also want to meet with Asher, the department chair, after doing his homework about switching mentors within the department. But first, Noah should find out whether this has happened before in the department within the last five years and review a list of possibilities before scheduling an appointment with Asher. Noah must be well prepared for this meeting with Asher, so he will need to learn how the chair negotiates and be prepared for Asher's probable responses.

Possible Approaches

 While Noah still has three years left on his career development award, he could "tough it out" and look for a new laboratory at the end of several years, even if that meant leaving his current department. But he would still need to try to preserve his relationship with Danielle, probably both personally and professionally, to make it work over the next three years. After all, Noah has put a tremendous amount of energy into this relationship over several years. And perhaps he is somewhat responsible for not trying to negotiate each issue in a more collaborative fashion.

As an alternative, Noah could go directly to Asher, plead his case, be assertive, demonstrate his value to the department, and see what happens. Or Noah could confront Danielle directly and try to negotiate a new relationship, seeking to reduce his reliance on her and moving more quickly to a colleague-colleague relationship. Noah also needs to get full, not just junior, membership in a number of academic societies. Both of these strategies—taking his case to Asher or demanding that Danielle rethink their relationship—would require a competing, assertive style. He will need to prepare his arguments very carefully, thinking about how to frame them, and even practice these before the meeting. (A quick review of strategies from Chapter 4 would be in order.) Whatever he decides, Noah will need to consult with other colleagues in his department, including senior members, to figure out the best approach, both short- and long-term.

Outcomes

 After assessing various outcomes and doing all his homework and meeting twice with the chair, Noah could decide to continue with Danielle. Perhaps he sets up a schedule of six-month goals and work products and will meet with Asher every six months to assess his progress. Noah pursues this road and focuses on collaborating with Danielle—even though he is concerned how this will work out.

One outcome could be that after several frustrating meetings with Danielle over 12 months, Noah decides to apply for a faculty position elsewhere. This is still a reasonable tactic, since he has two years left on his career development award. Finally, another alternative is that everyone agrees that it would be best for Noah to have a new mentor in the department—a change that could be carried out promptly. If this happens, Noah could find that his new mentor strongly supports his work.

Lessons

In looking at his situation, Noah realizes that he should have done a much better job of recognizing the inherent difficulties of communication and his own failure to appropriately negotiate the changes that were occurring in his relationship with Danielle. A range of negotiating skills would have been extremely helpful in not letting things fester and allowing the relationship to become contentious. He should have consulted other junior and senior colleagues much earlier in the process.

Noah also did not think through his choice of a mentor, mistakenly assuming that one mentor is all he needed. No matter how well things appear to be going, having at least one other advisor can be very useful, a move toward becoming more independent that everyone needs to negotiate sooner or later. Noah also should have done a better job of analyzing the pros and cons of breaking up with any mentor, and if he chose to sever the relationship, the timing of such a move.

Such a review can raise flags about the need to employ assertiveness and flexibility in continual pursuit of a career. Noah, in this situation, either did not see (or preferred not to see) that he needed to do more than avoid the problems in his relationship with Danielle. He also probably did not demonstrate enough creativity and flexibility in working out the details of his initial faculty contract. Putting all his professional eggs in one basket proved to be a very bad idea.

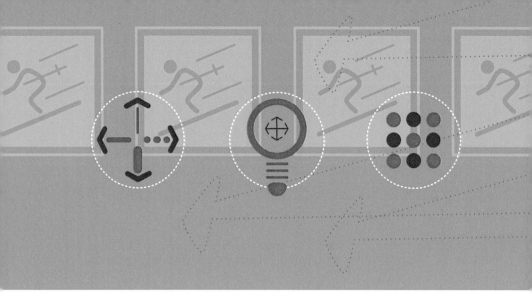

CHAPTER 16
First Faculty Appointment

Scenario

It's finally show time.

Lilah has been waiting patiently for this stage of her career, which she knows is a key step in her professional trajectory. After years of studying, working, and assisting professors, Lilah is ready for her first faculty position.

She's off to a fair start: three of the eight universities Lilah applied to responded by asking her to visit, which she has done, to discuss a three-year contract. At each school, she was asked to give a talk at a departmental seminar. The research seminar on her own work and the future directions of her research went well at the first two universities, and faculty members at both places are optimistic that Lilah will receive a job offer, even without a second visit. Things were not so rosy at the third university, the most prestigious on her list; Lilah knows she could have made stronger impressions in several meetings with individual faculty members throughout the day. Unfortunately, this third school is her first choice, a place where she knows she could grow and learn and also make a national reputation for herself more quickly than she might elsewhere. What should Lilah do now?

Preparing for the Context

 As Lilah assesses these options, she realizes she is not sure how to make the "best choice." If she gets no job offers, of course, she won't have any choice to make. Getting only one offer wouldn't be too difficult, since she would be pretty silly not to accept it. It wouldn't be the first time in her career that Lilah has had to make accommodations.

Now Lilah reluctantly realizes she may have to evaluate carefully the short-term and long-term consequences of her decision. She tries to see the situation through the eyes of those doing the hiring at each university: they need a young faculty member to fill teaching and committee obligations, and in return they will give her a chance to conduct research and try her luck at obtaining external grant funding. If she succeeds in getting grants and doing cutting-edge research, the university will benefit, both in prestige and perhaps new dollars. To really see things this way, Lilah will need to exercise considerable social intuition.

If Lilah takes a step back and looks at her own situation in a larger context, she has invested many years in school, training, doctoral, and post-doctoral experiences, and now it is time to get a "real job." She needs to start paying off her college loans (luckily, she took advice from colleagues and did not take out any loans for grad school), and she is considering getting married, all of which will be much easier with a good salary. All this pressure makes her realize that if she does get an offer, accommodation is the best road. If she gets more than one offer, she will have to weigh all her options carefully and, if she really wants to get to the best possible place, she will need to be assertive.

LILAH'S GOALS

Issue	First Faculty Appointment
Other Parties	All the individuals Lilah encountered on her three university visits; her Mentor; her Advisor, and Colleagues at her current school

GOALS	ACTION
Specific	Talk to at least three peers and advisors for guidance about job transitioning
	Create a list of negotiable items that she would like in her new job position. Lilah's focus should center on: starting salary, lab space, lab personnel, and starting lab salary. Lilah needs to begin to narrow her options based on her previously determined priorities in choosing the job that is right for her
	Be prepared to disclose these goals with people at the universities she is negotiating with
	Create a time frame for deciding what job she'll accept and a deadline for completing the hiring process
	Make a final decision by the time the hiring season ends
Aspirational	Plan to ask at the high end for her justified start-up package cost and salary
Reasonable	Some universities may not be prepared to offer all that she asks
	Because of conflicts between what Lilah is asking for and how the university's program is structured, a particular university may not work out
	Lilah should remember that there will be pros and cons to each place and that she might have to be more accommodating in some situations or negotiations than in others
	Some institutions might respond more quickly than others

Assessing the Counterpart

Lilah's situation has many variables and many players, with possible counterparts at each university in the roles of faculty members, hiring committee members, department chairs, and even future colleagues, and assessing them all will take considerable time and energy. Because her choice may well involve trade-offs, Lilah will want to be clear with herself about the pros and cons of each place and make a systematic analysis of all her options. Each conversation with a university is like a different trail, and learning more about each trail will make them easier to navigate.

To do this, she will want to set clear priorities for her personal and professional life, asking questions such as: Which of the three institutions has the best track record in terms of their junior faculty's success? What is the best compensation package that has been available for junior faculty? What is the cost of living in each of the three settings? How close does Lilah want to be to her family? What does she need as a start-up package for 1) salary commensurate with her rank and the local cost of living; 2) administrative/secretarial support; 3) adequate space, especially if laboratory work is involved; 4) personnel such as doctoral students and research assistants; 5) equipment (if laboratory work is involved, exactly what equipment will Lilah need for her own use, and what will be shared with other faculty and staff?); 6) opportunities to attend relevant meetings outside the university; 7) the length of the university's commitment to Lilah, including how long she will be expected to bring in grant money and how long she will be able to work without having to get funding. For this time commitment, Lilah will need to know what specific expectations each department chair has. For example, what is the breakdown of teaching responsibilities, administrative and committee activities, and research time (and if clinical training is involved, the time commitments for clinical work and research time)? Each of these questions needs to be examined and ranked in importance.

Possible Approaches

As Lilah reviews the various possibilities of a faculty position, she will have to try to assess her current situation. Because each of the three academic jobs offers only a three-year contract, this move does not necessarily represent a lifelong commitment, so perhaps Lilah should concentrate on getting offers from the first two places. Another strategy is to contact all three universities about scheduling a second visit. And Lilah can also reach out again to the universities that did not respond at all to her first inquiry.

Outcomes

Lilah completes this analysis and then contacts each of the three institutions to get answers to all her questions, explaining that more information will help her make a good decision. Two of the three universities, including the one where things did not go as well as Lilah had hoped, take their time in responding, but the first school Lilah visited responds quickly and provides answers to almost all her questions. The hiring committee members at the first school invite her back for a second visit, which includes a cordial meeting with the departmental chair, and Lilah receives an offer that contains most of what she asked for, one clearly forged out of trying to craft a solution that would work for everyone involved. Lilah was flexible about what would make her happy and was collaborative in working out the university's offer.

Now what should she do? One possibility is to take the first university's offer. She may not get another; the job market is not great, and this will be Lilah's first job, one that gives her enough research time to look for grant funding. But it is also just the first offer. Might a second one be better? Can she wait? The university wants an answer from her within a month, preferably within two weeks.

Knowing she has at least two weeks and knowing how important this choice is, Lilah contacts the other two universities again, lets people there know she has received one offer, and reminds them she is trying to complete her job search within two months. If she is a serious contender for a faculty position, Lilah says, could they let her know this (and any details about the position that they can give) soon? Three weeks later, she receives an offer letter from the second university. But comparing the offers is a challenge: The second one is vague and indicates that she does not need to make a second visit before deciding about the offer, essentially saying "take it or leave it." From the third, prestigious university: nothing.

Lilah still ponders how to make a final decision. She tentatively decides to opt for the first, complete offer but asks people at that university to give her two more weeks to respond. Even though she is happy about the terms of the first offer, she decides she needs to clarify several more issues, particularly staff support and the start-up equipment budget. The departmental chair, who clearly wants her, agrees to these additional requests, and the information-exchange process continues for several months before Lilah finally signs on at the first university.

Lilah knows that because delaying her response might make people wonder about her commitment to and interest in the university, she needs to tread firmly but lightly, being patient, persistent, and gracious. She does so by continuing to be assertive—but framing her persistence as a way to ensure that her work will benefit both the department and the university.

Lessons

Like most long learning experiences, this one was challenging and stressful but also educational. Lilah learned that being assertive is not the same as being aggressive and that she could and should push gently to get what she needs. She also knows that she should have consulted others, both peers and senior advisors at her current university, more than she did. Although she felt uncomfortable asking some of them about her plans to leave, in retrospect that would have been useful. Next time around, Lilah will remember that more information can help her make a better decision.

CHAPTER 17
First Grant Award

Scenario

Daniel's first thought was "I can't believe I get paid to do exactly what I want."

Daniel joined the faculty at a small West Coast university on a three-year contract, his first faculty job, 18 months ago, and he has just learned that he has received a basic neuroscience grant from a national research private foundation with direct-cost funding of $100,000 for each of the grant's two years.

He's pleased and proud all at once: the grant was awarded after a prestigious national competition specifically limited to young investigators, and because only one person could apply from any one institution, Daniel's selection makes him a kind of poster boy for his university. Following the advice of other faculty members in his department who have gotten grants, Daniel immediately made an appointment with Alexis, his department chair, to share the good news and go over the specifics of the new laboratory setup he will need to carry out the grant.

At the start of that meeting, Daniel carefully laid out the details of the new grant for the next two years and asked for additional lab space, one new research assistant, and a half-time administrative assistant. After congratulating Daniel for winning the grant, Alexis said that unfortunately her hands are tied: the department negotiates its budget with the university only once a year, and all money for the year to come has already been allocated. She would, she told Daniel, be happy sit down with him in seven months, when the new budget is being prepared, to talk about what's possible. But for now, he can't have an extra cent.

Daniel had to struggle not to show his huge disappointment—he actually wanted to get up and leave the room immediately—and instead managed a look that he hoped showed surprise. Has this ever happened to another faculty member, he asked? Could Daniel and Alexis set up a time to talk in the next few days, in hopes of starting to look for solutions together? Despite the fact that Daniel was in a state of mild shock, he was able to shake hands with Alexis, smile, and end the meeting cordially.

Preparing for the Context

 After going for a long walk in the local park, Daniel feels less acutely upset and begins to assess the situation. (Knowing when and how to take a break to reassess is an important skill for any negotiator, so think now about what kinds of action or activity calm you down and help you think—walking? talking with a relative or friend? doing a crossword puzzle?—and remember to stop and do that when you feel pressured or stressed.) After only 18 months in the department, he has received a big grant, one with a highly competitive national selection process. The good news is that he got the grant; the bad news is that he has only 18 months left on his initial three-year contract.

Before he can do any good negotiating, Daniel really needs to know how other junior faculty have dealt with getting similar grants—especially unexpected grants—in the middle of the university budget cycle over the past five years (which is a reasonable time frame for appropriate comparisons). This information will help him enormously, perhaps allowing him to understand Alexis' perspective and giving him ideas for solutions to his own predicament.

As he carries out his departmental fact-gathering, however, Daniel learns that the department has been conducting a big recruitment drive in the past three months—an effort that, according to rumor, has eaten up most of the department's current fiscal reserves. Daniel's research also unearths the fact that according to reliable sources, Alexis will step down in 18 months. This is not yet public knowledge, but Daniel trusts the people who told him to know what's up.

Daniel is not angry, but he's not pleased, either. He should be celebrating, drinking champagne, but all he can do is have a couple of beers while trying to figure out how to reopen this negotiation.

DANIEL'S GOALS

Issue	First Grant Award
Other Parties	Alexis, Daniel's Department Chair; Faculty Members; Colleagues who have been in Similar Situations

GOALS	ACTION
Specific	Daniel needs to: Talk to Alexis again about his grant Identify and explain his needs, focusing on lab space, a new research assistant, and a half-time administrative assistant Make a detailed list of what he needs and why he needs it to successfully complete his grant project
Aspirational	Perhaps Alexis will try her best to help him complete his grant, meeting his needs Daniel should still ask for all his goals and push to get them
Reasonable	Daniel should: Find out how others have handled similar situations Remember that Alexis is bound by certain protocols and regulations, and he might have to be patient in reaching his goals

Assessing the Counterpart

 Analyzing what to do and what options are best requires a lot of detective work. To find out what has happened in the last five years, Daniel will need to speak to a range of faculty members. He may find it easiest to talk with his peers, but they may be reluctant to share all the details of their own experiences. Senior faculty may be more helpful, especially if Daniel has already developed a relationship with them. Sometimes, staff involved in the grants office of the university have excellent insights into the process of acquiring resources. Because Daniel knows he cannot function well without adequate resources if he wants to establish an independent research career, he should talk with colleagues in other departments within his own university—or in similar departments at other schools—about similar experiences. Surely he is not the only one who has been caught in this budgetary fix: if Daniel is one of only four US researchers who got this award this year, why not find out how the other three negotiated the initiation of their grant in their respective departments? As always, understanding Alexis's track record is essential. How has she handled such challenges in the past? If she is headed out the door, might she be feeling more lenient?

Possible Approaches

 Daniel should congratulate himself on how he ended the meeting with Alexis. Buoyed by his good news, he certainly hadn't been expecting a flat, if cordial, "no" from Alexis, and he did well to hide his dismay. Surprises happen all the time, and often the best response is to leave cordially (if still in shock) instead of trying to negotiate when you are not ready or when you are so angry you might say something you will regret. Consider this a good and smart use of avoiding. (If he had had more time and an inkling of what was ahead, Daniel could have discussed some of his grant details with colleagues, especially senior ones, before sitting down with the chair, which might have given him a little insight into Alexis' probable response and spared him a nasty surprise.)

Daniel's first thought is that Alexis' response to his getting such an important grant is totally unacceptable. He was counting on being able to receive this grant, and any delay in starting the work will put him well behind schedule for his initial faculty appointment plan and goals. Daniel is so upset that he considers threatening to leave as well as going public, openly discussing the unsatisfactory situation with others inside and outside the institution. Another alternative is to use the time between now and the next budget proposal to carefully prepare his case for additional resources. A third choice would be to avoid any "big" trouble and seek guidance from Alexis about what to do in the meantime.

Daniel does not want a bruising battle with the administration at a time of change, but instead of avoiding (his primary modus operandi), perhaps he should use his best empathy skills and demonstrate the right degree of assertiveness to pursue a collaborative solution for himself. Getting down this intermediate trail will require a good bit of energy, but the outcome may be worth it. Daniel needs to see Alexis again and find out what she can do to help the department even more than she is now.

Outcomes

After assessing all the issues, Daniel sees one possible outcome as making a second appointment with Alexis, expressing his disappointment with her decision, and letting her know that he is considering beginning to look for a new job immediately. He also could tell Alexis he plans to let officials at the foundation know about the difficulty he is experiencing in initiating the grant, especially since the institution did "guarantee" that the available resources would be in place to conduct the grant. If Daniel proceeds along these lines, he clearly would be moving into competing and using his leverage (the grant and its prestigious reputation).

While considering this option, Daniel spends some time with other faculty in the department and gets their "read" of the situation. But as he begins to consult with others, including members of other departments, he starts to worry that this is all going to get back to Alexis and that she will write him off and simply refuse to invest any more time or energy in him.

Before he has too many more conversations and much more time passes, Daniel should find out how Alexis has dealt with similar situations—and how she views those who disagree with her decisions or ask her for reconsideration. Naturally, lying low and waiting for the next budget cycle is another tactic, but this does not fit with Daniel's personality. He thinks waiting more than half a calendar year would be a colossal waste of time, and he also sees that avoiding any more negotiation now would not help his ability to negotiate future matters. So it becomes clearer that Daniel should try to collaborate with Alexis and develop a longer-range plan, including seeking out the new chair whenever that person is so designated.

Lessons

Daniel had assumed that a department chair would greet news of a big grant with pleasure—and would quickly switch to helping a young faculty member get to work. Instead, he learned that he was not the center of the universe and probably had to take a back seat to another project (in his case, the department's recruitment effort). He also learned, firsthand, about departmental politics. With better mentoring, more experience, a higher degree of empathy, and even some stronger social intuition, Daniel might have anticipated Alexis' less-than-gratifying response.

In the end, however, Daniel's collaborative (and Alexis' compromising) approach bore fruit. After a second meeting, Alexis agreed to get Daniel some temporary space and equipment for six months and promised to fully support his project the coming year. She also told Daniel that she was planning to step down and cautioned him about his future in the department, noting that the university dean was urging the department to go in a new direction and would probably recruit a new chair to make that happen—information that will be very important for Daniel to factor into any future decisions.

CHAPTER 18
Promotion and Advancement

Scenario

The time has come to move up.

Zach is two-thirds of the way through his second three-year contract at a medium-size college in the mid-Atlantic states. Mindful that many schools limit such contracts to two, he has begun to look ahead—and up.

He already has one solid option: after letting it be known at an important national meeting last month that he might be on the job market, he and the department chair at an excellent Midwestern university had an unsolicited and interesting email exchange, and shortly afterward, Zach was delighted to receive a confidential offer letter from the university. The offer is for a four-year position as an associate professor, a base salary of $135,000, and a laboratory start-up package of $750,000 over four years.

Thinking that this offer may be as good as he can get, Zach has visited the university twice in six weeks. He enjoyed meeting potential colleagues on the faculty, and on the phone recently, Zach virtually told his contact there that he is planning to accept the job. Although he hasn't signed anything formal, Zach hears from the local grapevine that administrators at his current school have learned about the Midwest offer, although the grapevine didn't say how they took this news. If they are angry, he may have to leave anyway. But maybe this offer will show his worth?

Then, just as Zach was starting to think about moving and settling in the Midwest, he got a call from the chair of a search committee at an Ivy League university who said the committee members are trying to lure bright young faculty into a new endowed position of associate professor, and she thinks Zach has a good shot at getting it. Zach never thought he could get a job at such a top-notch university, and the position the search committee chair outlines certainly sounds like his dream position. If Zach will send her the Midwestern university offer, this woman says, the search committee will review it—and match it.

Preparing for the Context

 Once his euphoria over the call subsides, Zach decides to reflect more systematically on his last two academic years. During that period, he has completed one very exciting project, presented the findings at a by-invitation-only national symposium, and from that research wrote two articles, as senior author, that were published in *Science* and *Nature*. This is a huge break, and he knows he needs to assess how he can leverage it.

Is negotiating his next job with two (or maybe three, depending on how his current school reacts) institutions at the same time too much of a risk? Zach knows that temperamentally he has never been a big risk-taker, but he realizes that if he is going to achieve his goals, more than a little assertiveness will be required. If he uproots himself now, he definitely does not want to move again anytime soon—certainly for 10 or 15 years—so how can he be sure his next step is the right one? He realizes that because not all institutions have the same scientific and political agendas, he needs to investigate tenure possibilities at each place.

As he reviews his options, Zach must analyze the strengths and approaches of each institution, including his own, as well as his potential "boss" in each place. For the past five years, he has enjoyed having as his advisor a very helpful senior faculty member who specializes in Zach's own area. The Midwestern university, he knows, just received a multimillion-dollar gift to establish an interdisciplinary center in Zach's overall area of research. Faculty and administrators at that school want to move quickly and are now recruiting six new faculty members to develop the center, which will be led by a senior scientist who has not yet been named. The Ivy League university, on the other hand, has the history, prestige, and resources of an old institution with a huge endowment. According to the search committee's chair, Zach would be directly reporting to the chair of the department.

Tenure is a big concern: What's the likelihood that Zach would get tenure (and therefore not have to move again in a few years) at the Midwestern school? Could a three-year appointment there put him in an even better negotiating position for a more senior position elsewhere? Zach's area of science is highly competitive, and the field is moving quickly. Interdisciplinary groups such as the Midwestern university center could have a definite edge in attracting outside private and federal funding.

ZACH'S GOALS

Issue	Promotion and Advancement
Other Parties	All The Relevant Players at Each School

GOALS	ACTION
Specific	Zach should: Find out what people at his current school are thinking about his offer from the Midwest university; are they inclined to make a bid to keep him? Choose one of two (or three) potential universities as his next workplace: the university in the Midwest, the Ivy League university, and perhaps his current institution Consult with advisors about any ethical issues connected to sending the confidential offer letter to the Ivy League school search committee chair Decide whether to send the letter Determine exactly what each school's offer includes List relevant details Prioritize his interests Consult with his advisors to determine the best steps in accepting potential job offers from outside universities
Aspirational	This is probably a long-term decision, so Zach needs to aim for the best financial package from a top-notch school Having multiple offers can give him leverage
Reasonable	Zach should: Understand that some universities might be more responsive than others Realize that he might have to accommodate more to get a prestigious position (in other words, the offer from a less impressive school might be much better than that from a top-notch university) Remember that others, notably those at his current school as well as those at the Ivy League and Midwestern universities, are involved in this situation Realize that if he chooses not to disclose information to his current bosses, they might be upset with him and his reputation could be damaged Be mindful that if people at the Midwestern university find out that he sent their offer letter to the Ivy League university, they could rethink the offer or even withdraw it-once again, Zach's reputation could be at issue

Assessing the Counterpart

 In this black-diamond negotiation involving high stakes, multiple players, and professional reputations, if Zach wants to have maximum flexibility to make an informed decision, he will need as much relevant information as he can gather. Assessing all the variables is something that he can do only by visiting the Ivy League university and the Midwestern one for several days each. If staying at his current school is an option (something Zach still needs to find out), he should step back and look at his current workplace as if he were an outsider considering moving there, so he can compare all three schools fairly and completely.

He needs to know a lot about each place: what generally happens to mid-level faculty members with respect to tenure and promotion? What is the cost of living in each area? How interested in Zach and his work do leaders of each university seem? What are the tenure and grant structures? Which departments seem most innovative or are good fits for Zach's research? Throughout this process, Zach will want to keep his focus on his priorities and remember that because of the confidentiality of his first offer letter, his reputation could be at stake.

Possible Approaches

 In reviewing this rapid stream of events, Zach should take time to address several big questions. First, how ethical is sharing the terms of the Midwestern university's offer with another school without the permission of those who sent it? Just because the second school, the one with ivied halls and the huge endowment, has a long and storied history, does not warrant violating one's personal sense of what constitutes ethical behavior. Also, even if people at Zach's current institution are angry because he has been looking elsewhere, perhaps he should be more open and engage them to see whether they are interested in keeping him after his contract ends. (In fact, before this new offer, they may have been expecting him to stay.) Should he try to visit the Ivy League university and talk to the department chair and faculty members before providing any information about his first offer or any terms his current university might come up with? Would life be simpler if he just accepted the Midwestern school's offer and skipped all the work and complicated negotiations connected to the other schools? Exactly how important is it for Zach right now, at this juncture in his career, to be assertive and get the best deal possible?

This last question is one Zach has already answered—by understanding that after his recent success with the articles in *Science* and *Nature*, now is the best time to be assertive and competitive (at least as competitive as he is comfortable) in pursuing his goals. If he finds that forwarding the confidential letter does pose ethical challenges, he will need to be assertive in conveying "no" to the Ivy League school about the letter while still conveying "yes" on his interest in the job. And if neither the Midwest nor the Ivy League university works out, Zach will want to keep his good reputation and work out a compromise with his current university. Now is not the time to burn bridges.

Outcomes

 Based on self-reflection and discussions with several close friends, Zach decides not to send the offer letter to the chair of the Ivy League search committee and to be open about the Midwest school's offer with colleagues at his current institution, including his advisor. They all counsel him to tell his department chair about offers before he visits the Ivy League university, because such things rarely stay secret very long. (This is sound advice: Zach's current chair and the chair at the Ivy League school were grad school classmates who have remained good friends, so the news probably would have traveled before Zach even left the Ivy League campus.) Even without forwarding the precise terms of the Midwest university offer, in a visit to the Ivy League school Zach might be able to find out how closely people there are willing to match it.

Lessons

Whatever happens, Zach realizes that he has already gained much from this situation: he is learning to deal with uncertainly and see it as an opportunity. He is also doing a better job of assessing what others may want from him. With no rejections so far, Zach has been able to look into the future in a more comfortable and systematic way.

However comfortable, though, Zach ends up reconsidering his mix of goals and priorities, reassessing how flexible he wants to be and remaining mindful of his own reputation as well as that of his current university. Zach did visit the Ivy League school and was disappointed by his meetings there, especially his discussions with the department chair. The offer was sketchy—only a three-year appointment with the possibility of promotion but not a tenure track. Back at his own institution, Zach's advisor turned out to be supportive of his desire to leave and establish his own niche at another institution. Zach is glad that he took the time to listen to his advisor. She and Zach had been working on a two-site grant proposal for the following year. She appreciated knowing about his deliberations and even floated the idea of his new workplace being the second site for research.

On another visit to the university in the Midwest, Zach continued to get reassurance about the new proposed center and his own opportunities in it, and at a reception during his stay, he got to meet a major benefactor of the center who responded with great enthusiasm to Zach's description of the research he wants to pursue. This high-level interest was a big unexpected bonus, one that ultimately pushed Zach to accept the Midwest university's offer.

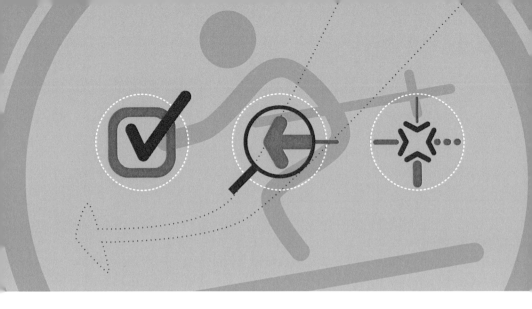

CHAPTER 19

Tenure

Scenario

From her perspective, Mika's future looks bright.

Now in her third faculty appointment at a large West Coast university, Mika is on the tenure track. She believes she has more than met the criteria for promotion to associate professor and tenure in her department: she started her first major research project three years ago and now has 20 peer-review papers to her credit, including 10 on which she was the senior author. Before she got the federal grant, she received funding from several foundations to pursue her research.

Some of Mika's senior colleagues have suggested she wait a year before going for tenure; by then, they note, her renewal grant will be funded and she may have several more published articles on her CV. Others, pointing out that relatively few women at Mika's university have tenure, especially in her department, say she should go for it now.

Preparing for the Context

Maybe, Mika thinks, this whole tenure thing is premature. Perhaps she should wait. But still, she tries to put it in perspective. Married, with two young children, Mika and her husband, Ian, need to decide soon whether to have a third child. Mika feels pressure and encouragement, especially from the women's faculty group, to go up for promotion. Ian was just transferred to another office, a lateral move in a local company, and both she and he are concerned about their family income. Although these realities have raised the temperature of discussions at home, Mika's husband remains very supportive of Mika's academic career.

Everyone can see that Mika's university is promoting more women and that its leaders want to see more women in the tenured and administrative ranks: the administration recently organized several seminars aimed at encouraging women faculty to assume larger academic and administrative roles, and the board of trustees just elected its first female chair. Members of Mika's own department are very interested in making sure the department is well represented within the university organization, so maybe the stars are aligned in her favor. The chair of Mika's department, Josh, has been generally supportive and says he will argue strongly on her behalf.

Younger associates in particular are urging her on: several post-doc women and one new female faculty member in her department are all encouraging Mika to go forward with the promotion process, knowing that her success could bode well for them and for the women who follow. Many of Mika's peers at other universities, women she studied with and has met at conferences, have already gotten tenure. When she looks at these women, however, she sees very busy people who travel often and are expected to take on new responsibilities in academic societies and organizations. A promotion would bring a raise, but is Mika ready for less time with her family? She knows that an important next step will be a discussion with her husband about this trade-off—a negotiation that could be just as challenging, in terms of setting goals and using skills, as her workplace ones.

MIKA'S GOALS

Issue	Tenure
Other Parties	Josh, Chair of Mika's Department; Ian, Mika's Husband; and Mika's Colleagues at her University and other Schools

GOALS	ACTION
	Mika needs to:
	Decide whether to apply for tenure now or next year
	Compile a list of advantages and disadvantages for applying now and applying later
Specific	Determine how other professors in similar positions got tenure–or what the common practice is for someone with her background in applying and accepting a tenured position
	Continue to gather information from her colleagues about what they think about her going for tenure now or later
	Begin assembling a dossier (if she decides to pursue tenure now) to present to Josh, her chair
	Why wait? Mika has worked hard and should get tenure as soon as possible
Aspirational	Mika has been a big contributor to the department's and the university's success over the years, and she should be confident in approaching Josh
Reasonable	Timing is a crucial element of almost all decisions. Sometimes people can't achieve their goals not because they lack talent or accomplishments but because of factors and realities beyond their control. Maybe university decision makers can't grant Mika tenure right now, but perhaps they can and will months (or a year) from now, at a time when Mika will be an even stronger candidate than she is today

Assessing the Counterpart

Mika knows that her next step is to make—and share with her husband—an honest assessment of what could happen in the next five years (once again, this is a reasonable time span to consider), including answers to several big questions. If she gets tenure, what kind of salary increase can she expect immediately? In years to come? Will having tenure enhance her chances of securing more departmental or university resources? As a tenured professor, will she have more independence in choosing committee or administrative responsibilities and assignments, the kind that can complicate the already-busy schedule of someone who must travel often to make her mark nationally? If so, how can she get guarantees of that independence within the department now, so future department leaders cannot renege on the arrangement?

These are some of the many questions any tenure candidate should consider—and they should all be addressed directly with a department chair. Getting answers will probably require more than just one conversation, and some of them will need written confirmation. Mika also should expand her reach within her own university and talk with senior faculty, especially women, in other departments. Finally, she will do well to gather information about comparable positions in other universities.

Possible Approaches

To continue working at her present institution while requesting a promotion, Mika will need a mix of assertiveness, empathy, and flexibility and a style that is more collaborative than competitive. Such an approach will help ensure that everyone involved (notably Mika, Josh, and senior faculty) is committed to one course of action and to the follow-through that will be required. It also sets a better tone for future work together and the next stage of Mika's career. Note that this approach still requires a healthy measure of assertiveness: once she decides to go ahead, Mika should prepare her dossier and show it to several senior advisors and members of the departmental promotion committee, including the chair of the department promotion committee, who is Mika's closest advisor and has served as a role model for her since she arrived.

After these discussions, Mika's next step should be to schedule an appointment with the department chair to review a five-year plan for herself, one that she has prepared after contacting colleagues at other schools and discussing comparable appointments. She may, as some peers have suggested, even seek out at least one outside formal offer, which could be useful in negotiating—collaboratively—a retention package.

Outcomes

 In many ways, this is a full-out campaign, one in which Mika has to decide how and when to carry out her strategy as well as keep her overall priorities in mind throughout the process. For something so important, this double-black-diamond trail, the prime style is likely to be a collaborative one, so Mika immediately begins working on her dossier and talks to people, those whom she might ask to write letters of evaluation, to find out what they think about her bid for tenure. She then schedules an appointment with Josh, letting him know the purpose of her meeting. She is pleased when Josh responds by encouraging Mika to bring a copy of her dossier, curriculum vitae, and a list of several recent publications to the meeting and when Josh accepts her offer to send him a draft of all the material before they actually talk. The meeting goes well, and Josh encourages Mika to go up for tenure now.

He says she will receive strong support from the department, but he acknowledges concern about the university-wide promotion committee that makes the final recommendation for promotion and tenure. But the following week, Mika gets a call from one of the associate deans for academic affairs, who meets with her and also encourages her to proceed. So far, so good, she thinks.

In the next two months, while her university's internal review continues, Mika gets a call from an associate dean at another university, one most people consider a strong competitor with Mika's current school. The other university has just established an endowment for promising women investigators, the assistant dean says, and he hopes Mika will apply for a new position. The university, he stresses, is keenly interested in promoting women.

Lessons

 Mika is surprised at what the last six busy months have surfaced: she has been forced to examine not just her hopes for the next five years but those for the next decade or more. She has had to think hard about balancing family and work—and the costs of any choice.

The outcomes are interesting in that she may have several choices at her current university—and now even some choices at another. After many conversations with her husband, she decides to seek tenure at her university now.

To her great pleasure, about the same time, Mika receives an offer from the second university, the one with the new endowment for female faculty, with an offer of tenure, a 25 percent increase in her current salary, and a substantial resource allocation for five years. She immediately lets her chair know about the offer and asks for his advice; he recommends that Mika ask for three months to consider the outside offer. Reluctantly, the other university agrees to the delay.

In those three months, Mika is heartened to see that her department supports her promotion package and "rushes" it to the university promotion committee, which approves her promotion to tenured professor. Now the decision is hers to make.

Mika and Josh quickly work out a five-year agreement on salary and resources that is comparable to the outside proposal, an arrangement he feels comfortable with because half of the actual contract package will come from a separate university fund, not from the department. This is a triumph of collaborative work, an effort in which both Mika and the department chair took enough time to craft a creative solution that was acceptable to everyone involved. The major lesson: Mika was prepared, flexible, and able to maintain focus as she worked her way through important negotiations for a secure future.

CHAPTER 20
Retirement

Scenario

What now?

Jed is still hale, hearty, and keenly interested in his work. But as he talks with many of his colleagues who are retired and living "the good life" (or so they say), he is wondering whether it's time to give up his tenured position.

He loves what he is doing, which is a combination of teaching, supervising, and doing some research. If departmental and student reviews are any indication, he's still very much in the game, receiving excellent reports every year.

But the department has just offered him a package to teach part-time. The salary would be considerably less than he gets now, but he would also have much less responsibility. The department chair, he knows, would love to use Jed's slot for a new hire. And Jed's wife would like to travel more, perhaps leaving the ice and snow of the Northeast for months at a time. She herself has recently retired. After all the help and support she has given him over the years, doesn't he owe her this much? What should he do?

Preparing for the Context

Jed has been a good departmental citizen, responding promptly and positively to requests to serve on or lead committees. Over several decades, he has arbitrated several complicated faculty issues. His teaching has consistently received positive reviews.

Yet while Jed would like to continue with the same level of activity, reflecting on his previous experience may be appropriate. Asking himself how the university and his department have worked with him over the 25 years that he has been with them, he wonders: have I been treated better than (or the same as) my colleagues? What have other tenured faculty (his retired colleagues and others) encountered when they reached retirement age over the past decade? How important is money?

Jed of course needs to look at the economy; today may (or may not be) a good time to cash out his retirement plan or pension investments. Years ago, when the US economy was in a slump, he would not have considered such a thing: all his pension benefits had suffered a significant hit, and hardly anyone in his university who had tenure was retiring. Even though his retirement plans have improved, almost to the level where they were years ago, Jed has to take a serious look at his family budget. If he retires now, he will certainly have more leisure time—but also less money to spend on the things he enjoys. He needs to review what is going on in his immediate and extended family.

All these concerns translate to an immediate need to revisit financial issues as Jed plans for the next 10 to 20 years. Has he directly gathered all information he can concerning pension and health benefits, either with full retirement or partial retirement as an immediate outcome? Are any of these benefits negotiable? Has he spoken directly and extensively with any colleagues who have retired in the past five years about their level of satisfaction? Has he asked them whether, if they had an opportunity for a do-over, they would have done anything differently? Has he consulted a lawyer or pension planner who specializes in working with academicians and has expertise in estate planning? Finally, has he considered moving to another university or taking a different job where he lives now, so he might not have to move?

JED'S GOALS

Issue	Retirement
Other Parties	Adam, Jed's Department Chair; Jed's Wife, Nomi; a Financial Planner and other Experts; Colleagues at Jed's University and Elsewhere

GOALS	ACTION
Specific	Jed needs to: Decide whether he wants to retire Find out what type of retirement package the university is offering and whether any terms of that package are negotiable Talk with his wife and determine how retirement will affect him and his family financially Create a retirement plan that works well with his university and his family Talk to friends and associates about how they transitioned into retirement and what advice they have. "If you could do it all over again," he should ask, "what would you change?" Respond soon to Adam, Jed's chair, who is pressuring him to retire. Jed needs to let Adam know whether he is inclined to stay on, retire, or transition to retirement Begin to develop a plan and agenda within the next few months (if Jed decides to transition into retirement) Provide Adam with a realistic plan soon (if Jed decides to retire now), so Adam can determine whether he can fill Jed's seat with a new hire
Aspirational	Adam recognizes all Jed's hard work throughout the years and helps him in every possible way Jed should ask for a generous retirement package and a timeline fitting his goals
Reasonable	Jed should understand that Adam and other university officials are not independent agents but are working with university staff and professionals Jed's retirement is hugely significant for him, but others may have to consider many factors in making certain compromises or accommodations–in other words, Jed has to recognize that there is a bigger picture here Jed is 72 years old. At some point, he's going to have to consider retiring

Assessing the Counterpart

 In this particular situation, although other approvals will need to come from the university administration, Jed's actual negotiation is with Adam, the chair of his department. The easiest choice appears to be accommodating the offer already on the table; doing so will certainly help the chair and ease the department's financial responsibilities. Throughout his career, Jed has prided himself on showing a great deal of empathy; he regularly agrees with and supports the department's leaders and is a strong candidate for any academic good-citizen award.

On the other hand, Jed knows this is his last hurrah, and he thinks maybe it is time to negotiate a better settlement using more of a compromising style. After reviewing the offers of the chair, Jed seeks to find a middle ground that does not adversely affect the finances of the department and still keeps his long positive relationship with the chair intact.

Possible Approaches

 This decision-making process raises new issues for Jed; he would have thought that in his long career he had seen and thought about almost everything, but he is surprised to be thinking now about how much his reputation means to him. In this, his last negotiation, how he plays and behaves really matters to him. After so many years in one place, he is inclined to compromise or collaborate. After all, there is time to analyze and find, in a problem-focused way, the best solution for all concerned. There is time to consider different viewpoints and use flexibility and creativity to come up with a solution that meets everyone's needs.

As he has done at so many steps in his career, Jed begins to weigh his options. One would be to continue what he is doing. He has a tenured position in the department and has served the university well. He is in good physical and mental health, has not slowed down, and is well liked by faculty and students. So perhaps there is no need to retire now.

But Jed wants to be sure he reviews all the possibilities. Another option is to negotiate a half-time position with continuing benefits and no administrative or committee responsibilities, which would allow Jed to continue doing what he really likes and give him and his wife, Nomi, time to get away from the harsh New England winter and develop new projects or hobbies. A third possibility is to work out the best possible retirement package before resigning and then resign. Being completely free of all university obligations does have its allure.

Outcomes

 After Jed gathers all the information he thought necessary, speaks to numerous colleagues, and spends time with a lawyer, financial planner, and family members, he seriously considers continuing his full-time position for another five years and then revisiting the idea of turning down the volume—but this would require his health to remain excellent and his department to support his choice. Jed notes, however, that the fiscal climate in his university is not great, and tenured faculty are under increasing pressure to retire. In two cases of colleagues he knows, this pressure took the form of demanding that they assume new responsibilities.

Since the university administration is pushing to reduce the number of older tenured (and expensive) faculty members, another alternative for Jed is to negotiate a part-time position with only the responsibilities that he likes. In fact, administrators may be interested in giving him a five-year contract if he is willing to give up his tenure. Finally, Jed figures, his last realistic choice, since he really does not want to move to another university, is to determine the best deal he can receive if he formally retires very soon. The negotiation of this retirement package may require hiring a lawyer, but that expense may be worth it in the long run. If he acts collaboratively and quickly, perhaps he and the university can reach an agreement and Jed will be able to leave the university in good fashion, possibly even with emeritus status.

The process of creating a solution that works for everyone takes six months, but it was time well invested. Jed, who had always worked 70 hours a week, had been understandably concerned about how he would adjust to his new life, but talking with many people within and outside the university helped set his mind at ease. He and Nomi worked with a financial planner to develop different scenarios based on his pension, social security, and several other assets. Armed with all this information, Jed met with the departmental chair three times, and together they developed a five-year plan. For the first two years, Jed would have a part-time faculty position and maintain 60 percent of his current salary. For the next three years, Jed would formally retire, become an emeritus professor and consult 10 percent of his time on various research projects. Everyone concerned felt that this was a reasonable solution.

Lessons

Jed's wish to make a graceful exit, to end his academic career in a good way, gave him a chance to reflect over the last 25 years and develop plans for the next two decades. Some surprising insights emerged: his reputation, he realized, has become increasingly important to him. He also realizes that this set of decisions about retirement is not as reversible or "fixable" as others earlier in his career. Asking for coauthorship or seeking promotion are all negotiations that can be revisited and reopened. This one, however, really was the last negotiation with his university. Extensive planning, he found, was hugely helpful and provided a strong foundation to negotiate a plan that works best for him, Nomi, and his family. He is happy to think that in departing, he could be known for graciousness, fairness, and loyalty.

CHAPTER 21
Back to You

Now we turn back to you and how others will perceive you in negotiation. This is not a question of your skill level or how you perceive, relate to, and understand those you are negotiating with. In earlier sections, we focused on all those areas, especially stressing the importance of empathy and social intuition. Instead, this chapter is designed to help you recognize your own culture, personality, and temperament (whether or not these are apparent to the other side) and understand how these can play out in a negotiation.

This might sound counterintuitive, but differences between parties in a negotiation can help you achieve what you want: different backgrounds can create different priorities, and different priorities can allow people to trade off items. Even differences in power or stature can make some negotiations easier. If you are negotiating for coauthorship with a much more senior colleague, for example, her need for first-author status might be much lower than yours. She is already a full tenured professor, after all, so perhaps she's more interested in mentoring you, getting this paper written before you complete your post-doc fellowship, and moving on to her next project. Your interests, on the other hand, might be getting the chapter done now (an interest you share with your colleague), having her name on the paper to give it prestige and get better journal placement (another shared interest), and having your name appear first, which will help on the job market (which of course is your own interest, although your senior colleague might also like to see you succeed). The differences in your status probably will make this negotiation easier than it would be for two junior faculty members coming up for tenure at the same time who both really want to be the first author on the article.

Sometimes, however, differences can stall a negotiation as you make cultural assumptions, verbal gaffes, and fail to communicate clearly because of differences. When you think about your negotiation patterns and assumptions, you can recognize how many different influences are at play. Of course, some differences, such as gender, race, and nationality, you can see and hear, and you might then incorrectly assume that these mean someone will always behave a certain way. When someone is especially assertive, is that because of his gender? His New York City roots, which you can hear every time he opens his mouth? But once you learn to look and think carefully, you'll see that less salient factors may explain his approach. Perhaps he is assertive because he was the oldest child, a high achiever who was told he could always have what he wanted. Perhaps he grew up in a neighborhood where being assertive was crucial to being accepted—or even to surviving. Perhaps he has had to be especially strong-minded and confident to thrive in his workplace.

Such assumptions can be even more pernicious when you look across cultures. Because you heard or read this somewhere, you might, for example, think (consciously or unconsciously) that "all Japanese say yes but really mean no" or that all scientists see the world in empirical terms, expecting things to happen in a timely, predictable way. Or that blondes have more fun. Beware such assumptions; like most general proclamations, they are often wrong.[81]

At the same time, being aware of some cultural norms is crucial. Putting your shoes on the table, for example, can be offensive to some. In some parts of the world, even a gesture as apparently benign as "thumbs up" or a practice as common as tipping a taxi driver can be insulting. But as with other differences, remember that any cultural rule is, at best, only generalizable to a plurality of that culture. When you are negotiating with a particular German scientist or a particular Spanish professor, for example, you have no idea how much of her national stereotype she adheres to—or how much her birth order, family size, professional training, social class, economic background, or inherited temperament has affected her negotiation behavior.[82] Perhaps she has lived in the United States for decades and has essentially become assimilated. For all these possible reasons, the ethos in one lab might not reflect any one culture but might instead be a mix of all of the cultures its scientists come from.

In thinking about the differences among negotiators, you may want to look back at the negotiation skills described in earlier chapters to understand how these differences might be reflected in those skills. Seeing how cultural, gender, regional, professional, and other differences can be reflected in negotiation skills should be a two-way mirror—are there certain behaviors in negotiation that you engage in based on any of these differences? Knowing where your behaviors come from (you watched your mother negotiate vigorously in the market every day; you were the middle child in a family of six; you were repeatedly told to "be nice" or that "if you can't say something nice, don't saying anything at all") can give you insight as you add to and build your skills. Similarly, as you negotiate with others, understand that visible differences (such as race, gender, and culture) may be more or less important than the differences you cannot see (and probably will not discover unless you ask).

Under assertiveness, differences in willingness to negotiate are sometimes ascribed to gender (women may be less likely to start or view something as a negotiation) or culture (Latin Americans or Europeans may be more comfortable bargaining, since they have more experience in markets). But this interest in sitting down at the table could also be ascribed to personality, levels of confidence, family dynamics, or work experience. Best practices suggest that you initiate negotiations when you need something, so thinking about how you do this—and how you judge others who start negotiations—can be helpful. Similarly, how assertive you are in the negotiation—how directly you ask for what you want, how long you talk before getting down to brass tacks, what tone of voice you use—all may have something to do with these differences.

Your framing and persuasion tools also are affected by differences. People from hierarchical cultures or high-status people in individualistic cultures might be more persuaded by appeals to their status or need for leadership. Your analogies to explain fairness might also differ depending on the culture of the person across the table. For example, "one cuts, the other chooses" (or "one divides, the other decides") as an explanation of a fair process will resonate far more with people who have siblings (or have watched children's television shows where these lessons are emphasized). Other persuasive strategies such as demonstrating common interests or similarities are best used only after you have figured out what you and your counterpart have in common. So even when you and the other negotiator do not look or seem similar, advance research or questioning can help you find shared interests. (Good salespeople know all about this—they find out as much as possible about the buyer, in hopes of finding common ground.) In science, look for common schooling, similar experiences with mentors, or even attendance at the same conference. When you find that commonality and talk about it, your counterpart will be more likely to listen to your arguments.[83]

The need to understand the other person in order to persuade ties into best practices in empathy as well. Your knowledge of his or her culture (whether you found this through advance research or by asking good questions at the table) will demonstrate respect and understanding. When you have an awareness of the other person's culture, background, and history, you will be more likely to understand where he is coming from and why he cares about some things more than others.

And yet we know that finding out about your counterpart is harder when there are differences. Be patient. Be curious. Ask open-ended questions. And be willing to share information about yourself. Remember those ice-breaking games (from school or workshops and trainings) in which you had to talk with strangers and find one thing you had in common? Consider putting this to use at the negotiation table (or before you get there). Try to find where you and your counterpart have similarities and differences that are not obvious. Even if the commonality or similarity is a seemingly minor one (you both have vacationed in South Dakota; you are both the middle of three children; you both detest tomatoes), recognizing and naming it will help build understanding. And when you discover differences, you will perhaps understand your counterpart, her behavior, and her motivations a little better. This more nuanced understanding will also keep you from jumping to conclusions too quickly about what is influencing her negotiation behaviors—gender, training, birth order, nationality, or none of the above.

The complement to this empathy is social intuition—the skill of putting others at ease, schmoozing, or applying social grease to get along. Cultures can vary widely in expectations for the stage known as schmoozing. What might seem endless small talk to one person is for another a crucial step in building connection. Stories abound of task-oriented Americans trying to talk business over a meal in countries where that behavior is seen as rude, so be alert for signals from your counterpart about how and when to chat—and when to shift to negotiating.

Your social intuition skills will need to be more attuned when your counterpart is different, as the assumptions you make might not automatically be correct. Similarly, recognize that the other person might be cautious about engaging, so don't necessarily interpret hesitation as disinterest or hardball—it might just be caution. Finally, your social intuition should be "on" for recognizing how others might see you. Like you, the other person will see—and perhaps respond to—salient differences. She might be aware of perceived status differences (your rank is higher, you went to a better school); regional differences, or class differences. Experienced negotiators work to make the other party feel comfortable regardless of these variances.

The skills directly tied to ethical behavior—guarding your reputation, being trustful and trustworthy—are deeply tied to culture. Just as you would expect your negotiation behavior to change based on the reputation of the person across the table, your behavior might also shift based on the reputation of the person's culture. Those shortcuts, also known as stereotypes, are needed to make sense of lots of information that you might have about different cultures. And as with all stereotypes, these reputations are also dangerous. Maybe the other person is assertive because he's a native New Yorker (or grew up in a tough neighborhood or once worked as a longshoreman). Or maybe not. Maybe your counterpart spends a lot of time on small talk because she's Italian. Or maybe not.

Stereotypes also come into play when you are deciding to trust your counterparts. You are more likely to trust someone who is like you—hence the importance of building connections, so that the other person will trust you and be less likely to deceive. To limit the opportunity for miscommunication and lack of trust, your assumptions about commitment and follow-through need to be even clearer when you are working with people from a different culture or cultures. Just think of the complexities involved in international diplomacy, whether leaders are discussing an economic bailout for Greece, a nuclear détente with Iran, or the search for peace in the Middle East—all of which are clear examples of the continuum of trust and distrust.

Flexibility—both in terms of process and outcome—is the skill that can bring all these differences together. Recognize that the other person's level of flexibility, from a little to a lot, may stem from his or her professional culture. Lawyers, for example, are trained to argue both sides of a case. Scientists, on the other hand, are trained to look for the right answer in a linear iterative fashion. A middle child may be more inclined to find the middle ground than the baby in the family. An only child may have had little experience compromising. Someone who grew up with very little money may believe that "giving in" is giving up. And so on.

When dealing with those who are different from you (as inevitably you will), remember that best practices in flexibility will help smooth the situation. Think of different ways to engage in the negotiation, different strategies for approaching the situation, and different outcomes that can accomplish your goals. By being acutely aware, observing differences and commonalities, and remaining flexible in how you communicate, you will be well prepared to negotiate and navigate whatever stretches out before you: easy slopes, sometimes-challenging routes, or dangerous black-diamond trails studded with surprises.

CHAPTER 22
Conclusion

No one is born knowing how to be a great negotiator. We called the first chapter of this book "Where you start" for good reason: We believe that the trail to becoming a consistently effective negotiator begins with self-awareness, some sense of which negotiation skills and styles you already have, use, or favor. To achieve your goals, you certainly need to recognize and understand the various styles of negotiation—competing, accommodating, avoiding, collaborating, and compromising—and mastering the skills of assertiveness, empathy, flexibility, social intuition, and ethical behavior is even more crucial to success.

As with so many other efforts, becoming an effective negotiator is a lifelong process. Negotiation skills are interpersonal skills. As you grow in how you assess yourself and others, how you plan and prepare for difficult meetings, and how you conduct yourself in those interactions, you will surely see growth across the span of your lifetime. This book focuses on more than self-improvement, but we do think that in reading it and thinking about all its ideas, you can learn a lot about yourself. And, as one of our colleagues put it, self-knowledge allows you to own your life and your career. With it, you really can decide what you want—or what you do not want—to do.

You have now read through the explanatory chapters, learning about various negotiation styles and the skills that matter most in difficult encounters, and have seen how these played out in the scenarios. How can you put all this into practice in your own career?

We recommend trying out your skills in a situation similar to one of the scenarios we sketched out in Chapters 12 through 20. Each time you use these skills in a real-life encounter you will be pushing yourself to improve, and you'll be well on your way to success. Another approach is to write your own scenario, following the structure we used: describe the situation; detail how you might approach the negotiation and its particular context; spell out your goals; assess the others involved; and critique your various options. Remember that if you really want to improve your negotiation skills, once you have finished negotiating, you'll have to be honest with yourself, willing to consider what went well, what did not, what was unexpected, and how you can do better in the future. This cycle of prepare, negotiate, review is truly the only way to continue to build your skills. Do remember, however, that because you can never have complete control over any situation, some things will not work as planned. Take that as well and learn from it. Try to treat surprises as opportunities to question your assumptions rather than setbacks.

Even if you are not a skier, we hope you will think about the analogy we've woven through this book. We started with a beginner slope, exploring the basic styles and skills that allow you to get down a hill without any major falls—in other words, to get through a straightforward negotiation without a major disaster. Then, as you reached later chapters and became more experienced and competent, you were able to tackle more complicated slopes, moving onto intermediate terrain. We hope that now, with more confidence in yourself and your ability to think ahead and accurately assess all the variables around you— the trail's conditions, possible hazards, and the weather, if you will—you might even be able to mentor and help others get down the mountain. As with skiing, becoming a consistently skilled, successful negotiator takes practice, insight, more practice, and review.

We wrote this book mostly from the perspective of the negotiator—you—and your counterpart or counterparts in today's culture. But keep in mind, as the chapter on communication styles notes, that how people exchange information is changing rapidly. Because today's devices allow almost-instant connection, first impressions take on huge significance and will probably become even more important as everything around us speeds up. Think long and hard about your first encounters; you may not have much of a chance to improve the impressions you make.

In this time of intense change, we think that the basic skills needed to negotiate effectively—assertiveness, empathy, flexibility, social intuition, and ethical behavior—will always be central to success. At the same time, we want to keep abreast of changes and are eager to hear your experiences, so please let us know what you think of the book and how you've put its ideas into practice. Our website, where we hope to feature new scenarios and help people continue to grow as negotiators, is smartsavvynegotiation.com.

We hope this book helps you achieve all your goals. Now get out there and enjoy the snow!

Smart&Savvy

NEGOTIATION STRATEGIES IN ACADEMIA

Appendix

FOR ADDITIONAL INFORMATION GO TO:

SmartSavvy**NEGOTIATION**.com

Scoring Sheets

Dynamic Negotiating Approach Diagnostic (DYNAD)

Scoring the Instrument

When you are finished, transfer the number from each item on the tally sheet. For example, on item A, if you selected number 6, write "6" on the line designated for item A on the tally sheet. Then add the numbers.

SAMPLE: B _1_ + H _4_ = _5_

Interpretation of the Instrument

1   This instrument gives you two sets of scores. Calm scores apply to your response to conflict when disagreement first arises. Storm scores apply to your response if things are not easily resolved and emotions and feelings of conflict get stronger.

2   The scores indicate your *preference*, or inclination to use each style. The higher your score in a given style, the more likely you are to use this style in responding to conflict. You can develop skills in the appropriate use of each conflict management style and, as such, are not limited to using the style(s) that you prefer.

Conflict Management Style Preferences - Tally Sheet

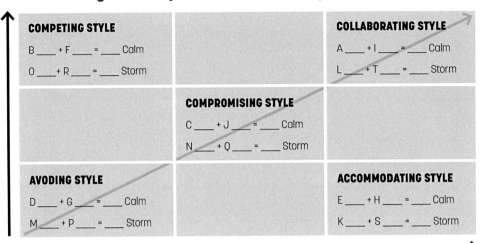

LEGEND

(Arrows read low to high)

Vertical Arrow: ASSERTIVENESS: Getting your own needs met

Horizontal Arrow: EMPATHY: Maintaining the relationship between yourself and the other party

Diagonal Arrow: The relative amount of effort and creativity needed to use conflict management style

Assertiveness

What the Test Means

The report on assertiveness examines your levels of boldness, outspokenness, and confidence. The higher you score, the more likely you are to know how to effectively and persuasively frame your argument while remaining calm and confident throughout the negotiation.

How to Score It

The **Assertiveness** scale is out of 64. Tally up numbers 1 through 16 and write your score here _____ to determine your **assertiveness score**.

10 to 25 You scored comparatively low on the assertiveness scale and may have difficulty with being assertive around others. You most likely find it difficult to voice your opinion or your interests during a negotiation. This also probably makes you feel taken advantage of or even unheard at times. Use the information in this book to learn more about what it means to be assertive and how to better reach your goals by being more outspoken and confident.

25 to 40 You scored moderately low on the assertiveness scale but show slight tendencies of assertiveness. You most likely have desires to state your mind but remain cautious about how it will be perceived by others. You may also have trouble being open about how you honestly feel in situations, and this may lead to your feeling frustrated with more assertive individuals, especially during a negotiation. Practice recognizing assertive behavior within yourself and make preparations to be more assertive in social settings and during future negotiations.

40 to 55 You scored moderately high on the assertiveness scale. You are likely knowledgeable of assertive behavior and have tendencies to exhibit assertive behavior in a negotiation. You do not shy away from the tough questions during a negotiation and feel comfortable when a conflict situation arises, as you see it as a challenge to overcome and conquer. Continue to gain knowledge on ways to be more assertive during a negotiation, to help improve your already assertive tendencies.

55+ You scored high on the assertiveness scale. You are well aware of assertive behavior and are frequently bold, outspoken, and confident in social settings. You most likely are enthusiastic about meeting new people or engaging in a new social situation. During a negotiation, others are well aware of your positions and the reasons behind them. This often results in your taking the lead on points during a negotiation and, for the most part, meeting your interests in most negotiation situations.

SOURCES
http://homepages.se.edu/cvonbergen/files/2013/01/A-30_Item-Schedule-for-Assessing-Assertive-Behavior.pdf

http://www.cengage.com/resource_uploads/downloads/0495092746_63633.pdf

Empathy

What the Test Means

The purpose of this report is to examine your levels of cognitive and emotional empathy. The higher your score, the more likely you are to better understand how to notice and respond to others' emotional experience during a negotiation. There are two categories for your empathy score

- Your level of **perspective-taking** shows how likely you are to understand another person's point of view.
- Your level of **empathetic concern** shows the extent to which you have feelings of compassion and concern for others.

How to Score It

The **Perspective-Taking** scale is out of 35. Tally up numbers 3, 4, 7, 9, 11, 12, 13 and write your score here _____ to determine your **perspective-taking score**.

10 to 15 You scored low on the perspective-taking scale for empathy. You have tendencies to ignore others' points of views and find it difficult to relate to their situation. You are likely to first determine whether a conflict is right or wrong based on your initial assessment and then may block out any other opposing opinions from others after your self-assessment. This may lead to others feeling angry and frustrated that you are "one-sided" or "narrow-minded." In the future, try to imagine yourself in the other's position when engaged in a conflicting situation.

15 to 25 You scored in the middle range on the perspective-taking scale for empathy. You are likely to understand another person's point of view and sometimes remain unaware of how others are feeling in a particular situation. Keep reminding yourself to understand where the other person's point of view is coming from. You can implement the skills and lessons learned in this book to better practice viewing information from another's perspective.

25+ You scored high on the perspective-taking scale for empathy. You are most likely able to recognize another person's point of view and are correctly able to identify his or her position. During a negotiation, other parties have most likely picked up on this skill and complemented your "good listening" skills. Continue to be aware of others' point of view during negotiations, as this encourages involvement and individual value of all parties at the negotiation table.

The **Empathetic Concern** scale is out of 35. Tally up numbers 1, 2, 5, 6, 8, 10, 14 and write your score here _____ to determine your **empathetic concern score**.

10 to 15 You scored low on the empathetic concern scale for empathy. You have difficulty recognizing and understanding the feelings and concerns of others. Try removing yourself from the situation and ask yourself, "How would I feel in this type of situation?" Force yourself to understand the emotions the other person feels and then, reflect on how those type of actions would make you feel in a similar situation.

15 to 25 You scored in the middle range on the empathetic concern scale for empathy. You have tendencies to feel compassion and concern for others and can also be unaware about the emotional concerns of others as they arise. When another party seems to be frustrated or upset on a position, try taking a mental break or pause to think about why he or she is feeling upset. Practice remaining aware of how others feel around you in social situations.

25+ You scored high on the empathetic concern for empathy scale. You have strong abilities for showing concern and being compassionate for people around you. This makes others around you feel "at ease" and "comfortable" during a negotiation.

SOURCES
http://fetzer.org/sites/default/files/images/stories/pdf/selfmeasures/EMPATHY-InterpersonalReactivityIndex.pdf

Flexibility

What the Test Means

The purpose of this report is to examine your levels of internal and external flexibility. The higher your score, the more likely you are to adapt to changing internal and external circumstances. There are two categories for your flexibility score:

- Your level of **internal flexibility** shows the degree to which you characterize yourself as flexible, open-minded, and innovative.
- Your level of **external flexibility** shows how positively you view change and whether you perceive reality as dynamic and changing.

How to Score It

The **Internal Flexibility** score is out of 30. Tally up numbers 4, 5, 6, 7, 8, 9 and write your score here _____ to determine your **internal flexibility score**.

10 to 15 You scored low on the internal flexibility scale. This means that you often do not change your mind on subjects. You are also not easily open to being flexible with yourself in social situations. You are most likely stuck in traditional or set-in-stone approaches during a negotiation and are not open to shifting your approaches. Reflect on the lessons learned in the chapter on flexibility and try to gain insight on how being flexible can help you achieve better outcomes during a negotiation. Then study the flexibility skills sections in this book to be more innovative and open-minded in future situations.

15 to 25 You scored in the middle range on the internal flexibility scale. You have tendencies to be flexible with yourself in social situations and also show signs of reservation when it comes to being open-minded or innovative. Believe in yourself and your ability to be flexible next time a situation arises where being flexible would be appropriate. Recognize that flexibility can lead to positive outcomes during a negotiation. Think about different ways you can be more flexible, open-minded, and innovative the next time a conflict situation arises.

25+ You scored high on the internal flexibility scale. This means that you are appropriately flexible when it comes to being open-minded and innovative with yourself. You most likely find it easy to adapt to situations as they occur in a negotiation, resulting in confidence and successful outcomes. Continue to understand different ways to be flexible in situations and self-reflect afterwards to better understand different ways you can be more flexible in social situations.

The **External Flexibility** score is out of 30. Tally up numbers 1, 2, 3, 10, 11, 12 and write your score here _____ to determine your **external flexibility score**.

10 to 15 You scored low on the external flexibility scale. You are most likely not comfortable with social change. You are more comfortable with strict structure and conformity. This means that when a negotiation begins to change in dynamics, you become tense or even withdrawn. Be open to participating in changing situations and environments. Review the lessons discussed in the chapter on flexibility and plan to incorporate them during your next negotiation.

15 to 25 You scored in the middle range on the external flexibility scale. This means that you generally view change as a good thing and also may be uncomfortable with change in some situations. As change begins during a negotiation, you are most likely optimistic about this being good. You may drag your feet as it happens as well. Remain optimistic and hopeful that reality can and often does change for the better.

25+ You scored high on the external flexibility scale. You are open to change and recognize that change is a constant part of life. You are happy to understand and tackle new obstacles as they occur. You remain optimistic and encouraged that change brings about new ideas, creativity, and solutions in an ever-changing world. This often causes others at the negotiation table to feel that you are fair-minded and concerned about their interests—leading to a collaborative negotiation agreement.

SOURCES

https://www.webmedcentral.com/article_view/4606

Social Intuition

What the Test Means

The purpose of this report is to examine your level of social intuition. The higher your score, the more socially intuitive you are. You can use this information to better understand how emotionally attuned you are to yourself and others and how well you use that knowledge to achieve your goals. By developing your social intuition, you can better adjust your own behavior based on the behavior of your counterpart—allowing you to monitor and shift negotiation styles strategically.

How to Score It

The **Social Intuition** scale is out of 10. Tally up numbers 1 through 10 and write your score here _____ to determine your **social intuition score**.

0 to 5 You have relatively low social intuition. You most likely have a hard time identifying social cues that indicate what others around you are feeling or trying to express. This often leads to stressful situations where you may not fully understand why a situation suddenly went south. Also, others may suddenly take offense to unconscious actions you took during a negotiation—such as speaking loudly, using sarcasm, or making impolite social gestures. Try to pick up on social cues such as body language, facial expressions, or whether a person looks tense or relaxed. Also try to be aware of how you are portraying yourself to other parties at the negotiation table.

6 to 10 You scored relatively high on the social intuition scale. You understand social concepts such as boundaries and recognize signs that indicate how others feel. You are most likely observant of other people's actions and can appropriately identify how others are thinking in the situation. In a negotiation you are able to shift the conversation according to social cues that you identify, leading to a smoother and more successful negotiation. You are probably also aware of how your bodily language affects others and are able to lead the negotiation based on your behavior during a negotiation.

SOURCES
http://www.scn.ucla.edu/pdf/Intuition.pdf

Style Advantages & Disadvantages

COMPETING

HIGH ASSERTIVENESS/LOW EMPATHY

"We're doing it my way ..."

Advantages

- Speed
- Decisiveness
- Preservation of Important Values
- Clarity

Disadvantages

- Harmed Relationships
- Loss of Cooperation
- Lack of Input or Feedback from Others

Best to Use in These Contexts

- When Need Quick Decision
- When in Charge and Expected or Needed
- When Key Values at Stake

Best to Use With These Counterparts

- With Accommodating to Get What You Want
- With Competing to Defend Yourself

ACCOMMODATING

LOW ASSERTIVENESS/HIGH EMPATHY

"OK, whatever you say ..."

Advantages

- Maintains Appreciation from Others
- Freedom From Hassle and Conflict (at Least in the Short Run)
- Defers to Others

Disadvantages

- Don't Get What You Want
- Frustration for Others Who Wish to Collaborate
- Loss of Respect From Others
- Denies Others Benefit of Healthy Confrontation

Best to Use in These Contexts

- When Issue is Not That Important
- When Relationship is Primary Interest

Best to Use With These Counterparts

- When Others' Interests are Primary
- When You Can "Bank" Accommodating
- With Other Accommodating Styles

AVOIDING

LOW ASSERTIVENESS/LOW EMPATHY

"Let's not make a big deal out of this ..."

Advantages

- Keep Your Focus on Other Interests
- Freedom From Entanglement in Trivial Issues or Insignificant Relationships
- Preservation of Status Quo

Disadvantages

- Periodic Explosions of Pent-up Anger (from you or at you)
- Residue of Negative Feelings
- Stagnation
- Loss of Accountability or Participation
- Does Not Build Relationship

Best to Use in These Contexts

- When Your Interests are Unimportant
- When You Don't Have Energy or Focus to Negotiate
- When You are Unprepared to Negotiate

Best to Use With These Counterparts

- With Competing to Negotiate Over the Rules
- When Not Engaging will Allow Others to Negotiate to Lead
- When Others Will Solve

COMPROMISING

MEDIUM ASSERTIVENESS/MEDIUM EMPATHY

"Let's find some middle ground ..."

Advantages

- Readily Understood by Most People
- Provides a Way Out of Stalemate
- Builds Atmosphere of Reasonableness Relatively Fast

Disadvantages

- Possibly Unprincipled Agreement
- Possibly Unprincipled Agreement
- Can Be Mediocre and Unsatisfying to All

Best to Use in These Contexts

- At the End of the Dispute to Bridge a Gap
- To Help Shift Styles at the End

Best to Use With These Counterparts

- To Move a Competing Style to Trading Off
- With Other Compromising
- With Accommodating to Give Them Something

COLLABORATING

HIGH ASSERTIVENESS/HIGH EMPATHY

"My preference is … I'm also interested in your views."

Advantages

- Builds Trust in Relationships
- High Cooperation & Compliance
- Merges Perspectives
- High Energy

Best to Use in These Contexts

- When Buy-in is Key to Compliance
- When Need Lots of Ideas
- When Want Team Building
- When Creative or Innovative Solution is Needed

Disadvantages

- Time Consuming
- Distraction From Other More Important Tasks
- Analysis Paralysis

Best to Use With These Counterparts

- With Other Collaborators
- With Competing to Move Them to Problem Solving
- With Compromising to Move Them To be More Creative

Endnotes

Chapter 1

1   Malhotra, D. 2014. 15 Rules for Negotiating a Job Offer. *Harvard Business Review* 92 : 117-120.

2   Schneider, A. K. and J. G. Brown. 2013. Negotiating Barometry: A Dynamic Measure of Conflict Management Style. *Ohio State Journal on Dispute Resolution* 28: 557.

Chapter 2

3   Blake, R. R. and J. S. Mouton. 1964. *The Managerial Grid: Key Orientations for Achieving Production through People*, 12th edn.; Thomas, K. 1976. Conflict and Conflict Management in The Handbook of Industrial and Organizational Psychology, edited by M. D. Dunnette. 889, 900-02. Chicago: Rand McNally.

4   Thomas, K. W. and R. H. Kilmann. 2002. *Thomas-Kilmann Conflict Mode Instrument Profile and Interpretive Report*.

5   Galanter, M. 2004. The Vanishing Trial: An Examination of Trials and Related Matters in Federal and State Courts. *Journal of Empirical Legal Studies* 1: 459-570.

Chapter 3

6   Freiling, T. 2009. *Walking with Lincoln: Spiritual Strength from America's Favorite President*. Revell.

7   John Wooden at the UCLA Anderson School of Management, John Wooden Global Leadership Award ceremony. May 21, 2009.

8   Fisher, R., W. L. Ury and B. Patton. 2011. *Getting to Yes: Negotiating Agreement Without Giving In*, 3rd edn. London: Penguin Books.

9   Shell, R. G. 2006. *Bargaining for Advantage: Negotiation Strategies for Reasonable People*. London: Penguin Books.

10 Schneider, A. K. 2017. Productive Ambition in *The Negotiator's Desk Reference*, edited by A. K. Schneider and C. Honeyman. St. Paul: DRI Press.

11 Shell, *Bargaining for Advantage*.

12 White, S. B. and M. A. Neale. 1994. The Role of Negotiator Aspirations and Settlement Expectancies in Bargaining Outcomes. *Organizational Behavior and Human Decision Processes* 57: 303-05.

13 Fisher, Ury and Patton, *Getting to Yes*.

Chapter 4

14 Korobkin, R. 2002. Aspirations and Settlement. *Cornell Law Review* 88: 1-61.

15 Tinsley, C. H., K. O'Conner and B. A. Sullivan. 2002. Tough Guys Finish Last. *Organizational Behavior and Human Decision Processes* 88(2).

16 Shell, *Bargaining for Advantage*.

17 Stone, D., B. Patton and S. Heen. 1999. *Difficult Conversations: How to Discuss What Matters Most*. London: Penguin Books.

18 Shell, *Bargaining for Advantage*.

19 Fowler, M. R. 2017. *Mastering Negotiation*. Durham: Carolina Academic Press.

20 Stone, Patton and Heen, *Difficult Conversations*.

21 Id.

22 Fisher, Ury and Patton, *Getting to Yes*.

23 Id.

24 Menkel-Meadow, C. 1999. The Art and Science of Problem Solving Negotiation. *Trial Magazine*, June, 50-1.

25 Tannen, D. 1986. *That's Not What I Meant: How Conversational Style Makes or Breaks Relationships*, 39-42.

26 Cuddy, A. 2012. Your Body Language May Shape Who You Are *TED Talk*. TEDGlobal.

27 Guthrie, C. 2009. I'm Curious: Can We Teach Curiosity in *Rethinking Negotiation Teaching: Innovations for Context and Culture*, edited by C. Honeyman, J. Coben and G. De Palo. St. Paul: DRI Press.

Chapter 5

28 Fisher, R., E. Kopelman and A. K. Schneider. 1994. *Beyond Machiavelli: Tools for Coping with Conflict*. London: Penguin Books.

29 Goleman, D. 2005. *Emotional Intelligence: Why It Can Matter More Than IQ*. New York: Bantam Books.

30 Lee, H. 1960. *To Kill a Mockingbird*. Philadelphia: J.B. Lippincott & Co. Publishing.

31 Barkai, J. L. 1984. How to Develop the Skill of Active Listening. *The Practical Lawyer* 30(4).

32 Wheeler, M. 2013. *The Art of Negotiation: How to Improvise Agreement in a Chaotic World*. New York: Simon and Schuster.

33 Freshman, C., A. Hayes and G. Feldman. 2002. The Lawyer-Negotiator as Mood Scientist What We Know and Don't Know About How Mood Relates to Successful Negotiation. *Journal of Dispute Resolution* 1.

34 Id.

35 Lewicki, R. J. and E. C. Tomlinson. 2014. Trust, Trust Development and Trust Repair in *The Handbook of Conflict Resolution: Theory and Practice*, 3rd edn. edited by M. Deutsch, P. T. Coleman and E. Marcus. San Francisco: Jossey-Bass.

Chapter 6

36 Lax, D. A. and J. K. Sebenius. 1986. *The Manager as Negotiator: Bargaining for Cooperation and Competitive Gain*. New York: Free Press.

37 Id.

38 Adler, R. S., B. Rosen and E. M. Silverstein. 1998. How to Manage Fear and Anger. *Negotiation Journal* 14: 161.

39 Ross, L. 1995. Reactive Devaluation in Negotiation and Conflict Resolution in *Barriers to Conflict Resolution*, edited by K. J. Arrow et al. New York: W.W. Norton and Company.

40 Fisher, Kopelman and Schneider, *Beyond Machiavelli*.

41 De Bono, E. 1985. *Six Thinking Hats*. New York: Little, Brown and Company.

42 Adler, P. S. 2006. Protean Negotiation in *The Negotiator's Fieldbook: The Desk Reference for the Experienced Negotiator*, edited by A. K. Schneider and C. Honeyman. Washington, DC: American Bar Association.

43 Brown, J. G. 2004. Creativity and Problem-Solving. *Marquette Law Review* 87: 697.

44 Menkel-Meadow, C. 2001. Aha? Is Creativity Possible in Legal Problem Solving and Teachable in Legal Education? *Harvard Negotiation Law Review* 6: 97.

Chapter 7

45 Mischel, W., E. B. Ebbesen and A. R. Zeiss. 1972. Cognitive and Attentional Mechanisms in Delay of Gratification. *Journal of Personality and Social Psychology* 21(2): 204-18.

46 Goleman, D. 2007. *Social Intelligence: The New Science of Human Relationships*. New York: Bantam Books.

47 Id.

48 Thompson, J., N. Ebner and J. Giddings. 2017. Non-Verbal Communication in Negotiation in *The Negotiator's Desk Reference*, edited by A. K. Schneider and C. Honeyman. St. Paul: DRI Press.

49 Pruitt, D. 1983. Achieving Integrative Agreements in *Negotiation in Organizations*, edited by M. Bazerman and R. Lewicki. 36-41. Thousand Oaks: Sage Publications.

50 Goleman, *Social Intelligence*.

51 Id.

Chapter 8

52 Lewicki, R. 2017. Trust and Distrust in *The Negotiator's Desk Reference*, edited by A. K. Schneider and C. Honeyman. St. Paul: DRI Press.

53 Welsh, N. 2012. The Reputational Advantages of Demonstrating Trustworthiness: Using the Reputation Index with Law Students. *Negotiation Journal* 28(1): 117.

54 Lewicki, Trust and Distrust.

55 Tinsley, O'Conner and Sullivan, Tough Guys Finish Last.

56 Id.

57 Id.

58 Id.

59 Johnston J. S. and J. Waldfogel. 2002. Does Repeat Play Elicit Cooperation Evidence From Federal Civil Litigation. *The Journal of Legal Studies* 31: 39.

60 Fisher, Kopelman and Schneider, *Beyond Machiavelli.*

61 Lewicki, Trust and Distrust.

62 Kahneman, D. and A. Tversky. 1995. Conflict Resolution: A Cognitive Perspective in *Barriers to Conflict Resolution*, edited by K. J. Arrow et al. New York: W.W. Norton and Company.

63 Reilly, P. 2009. Was Machiavelli Right? Lying in Negotiation and the Art of Defensive Self-Help. *Ohio State Journal on Dispute Resolution* 24(3): 481.

64 Id.

65 Menkel-Meadow, The Art and Science of Problem Solving Negotiation.

Chapter 9

66 Ebner, N., A. D. Bhappu, J. G. Brown, K. K. Kovach and A. K. Schneider. 2009. You've Got Agreement: Negoti@ting via Email in *Rethinking Negotiation Teaching: Innovations for Context and Culture*, edited by C. Honeyman, J. Coben and G. De Palo, 89-114. St. Paul: DRI Press.

67 Ebner, N. 2017. Negotiation via Email in *The Negotiator's Desk Reference*, edited by A. K. Schneider and C. Honeyman. St. Paul: DRI Press.

68 Thompson, L and J. Nadler. 2002. Negotiating via Information Technology: Theory and Application. *Journal of Social Issues* 58(1): 109-24.

69 Naquin, C. E., T. R. Kurtzberg and L. Y. Belkin. 2008. Email Communication and Group Cooperation in Mixed Motive Context. Social *Justice Research* 21(4): 470-89.

70 Nadler, J. and D. Shestowsky. 2006. Negotiation, Information Technology, and the Problem of the Faceless Other in *Negotiation Theory and Research*, edited by L. L. Thompson. Hove, UK: Psychology Press.

71 Bhappu, A. D., T. L. Griffith and G. B. Northcraft. 1997. Media Effects and Communication Bias in Diverse Groups. *Organizational Behavior and Human Decision Processes* 3(70): 199-205.

72 Morris, M., J. Nadler, T. Kurtzberg and L. Thompson. 2002. Schmooze or Lose: Social Friction and Lubrication in Email Negotiations. *Group Dynamics: Theory, Research, and Practice* 1(6): 89-100.

73 Ebner, Negotiation via Email.

74 Id.

Chapter 10

75 Thompson, L. L. 2005. *The Mind and Heart of the Negotiator*, 3rd edn. Upper Saddle River: Prentice Hall.

76 Sebenius, J. K. 2004. Mapping Backward: Negotiating in the Right Sequence? *Negotiation* 7, no. 6, June.

77 Doyle, M. and D. Straus. 1993. *How to Make Meetings Work!* New York: Berkley.

78 Fisher, Kopelman and Schneider, *Beyond Machiavelli.*

Chapter 11

79 Lee, A., C. Dennis and P. Campbell. 2007. Nature's Guide for Mentors. *Nature* 447: 791-797.

80 Adapted from Id.

Chapter 21

81 Rubin, J. Z. and F. E. A. Sander. 1988. When Should We Use Agents? Direct vs. Representative Negotiation. *Negotiation Journal* 4(4): 395-401.

82 Salacuse, J. W. 1998. Ten Ways that Culture Affects Negotiating Styles: Some Survey Results. *Negotiation Journal* 14(3): 221-40.

83 Guthrie, C. 2017. Getting Your Way in *The Negotiator's Desk Reference*, edited by A. K. Schneider and C. Honeyman. St. Paul: DRI Press.; Cialdini, R. B. 2001. *Influence: Science and Practice*, 4th edn. Boston: Allyn and Bacon.

Acknowledgements

We greatly appreciate the contributions of many individuals who helped us along the way in developing this book.

To the many participants and faculty of the Career Development Institute who enthusiastically clamored for more negotiation training over the years, we thank you so very much. Your continued interest in our work is what led to this book. To the folks at the 3C Institute in North Carolina, including Melissa de Rosier, Lauren Raab, and others with whom we have worked on negotiation videos and software over the years, your focus on how to educate adults has helped us clarify and hone our message.

We are also grateful to the many colleagues who read this book in early forms and provided excellent suggestions for how to improve the content and readability. While all remaining faults are ours, we credit Elizabeth Ellinas, Howard Gadlin, JoAnn Gora, Carol Liebman, Carrie McAdams, and Noah Philip for their helpful commentary and assistance. We are also truly grateful to Ellen Frank, wife and stepmom, who read multiple drafts and pushed us to collaborate. To Rodd Schneider, husband and son-in-law, who has continually encouraged the training that led to this book and pushed us to get this done, we are very appreciative.

We thank Louisa Williams and Todd Germann, respectively, for their outstanding editing and graphic design, and Carrie Kratochvil, Andrea's amazing administrative assistant, who effectively became an assistant to both of us.

Finally, to our children, siblings, and spouses: it is from you that we have learned the most about negotiation styles, long-term relationships, and the importance of collaboration. To show how important we think these skills are now and in the future, we have used the names in our family's next generation for the fictional individuals who negotiate their academic careers throughout this book.

— Andrea Kupfer Schneider and David Kupfer

Made in the USA
Middletown, DE
21 November 2017